Making Schools Work

Published in cooperation with
the Milken Institute
for Job & Capital Formation

Making Schools Work

A View from the Firing Lines

EDITED BY

Cheryl L. Fagnano and
Katherine Nouri Hughes

Milken Family Foundation

Routledge
Taylor & Francis Group
LONDON AND NEW YORK

First published 1993 by Westview Press

Published 2018 by Routledge
52 Vanderbilt Avenue, New York, NY 10017
2 Park Square, Milton Park, Abingdon, Oxon OX14 4RN

Routledge is an imprint of the Taylor & Francis Group, an informa business

A CIP catalog record for this book is available from the Library of Congress.

ISBN 13: 978-0-367-00914-4 (hbk)
ISBN 13: 978-0-367-15901-6 (pbk)

Contents

Preface

The essays in this volume are based on remarks and papers given at the third annual *Milken Family Foundation National Educator Awards Retreat* held in Los Angeles in March 1992.

Subsequently renamed the *Milken Family Foundation National Education Conference,* the gathering is the professional development component of the Foundation's National Educator Awards program. Conceived by Lowell and Michael Milken in the early 1980s, the program was formally established in California in 1987 and offers individual awards of $25,000 to professionals in elementary and secondary schools around the country. Its chief aims are to recognize and reward educators who have made and continue to make significant contributions to the education of children; to heighten public appreciation of the teaching profession thereby encouraging talented men and women to enter the field of education; and to contribute to the professional development of recipients by annually bringing them together with distinguished representatives of the profession and a range of public officials for a three-day conference exploring significant education issues. The program honors educators in each participating state, which in 1993 numbered 25.

Cheryl L. Fagnano
Katherine Nouri Hughes

Acknowledgments

The editors gratefully acknowledge the assistance of the following persons in the production of this book. David Weinrot and Sang Han provided the research support and computer wizardry for the analysis of the survey data in the final chapter. Laura Borns is duly commended for her patience in typing the manuscript through countless drafts, and always finding the time to make "just one more small change." Holly Hatch provided significant typing and proofing assistance. Lawrence Lesser, production director for the Milken Family Foundations, contributed the extensive technical expertise required to produce this volume. Laura Janssen's desktop publishing acumen delivered us from rough draft to polished copy. Finally, and most important, we wish to thank all of the Award recipients and the Retreat speakers whose energy and ideas made this book possible. They are among the brightest stars in America's schools today, and this volume is a tribute to their thoughtful leadership.

C.L.F.
K.N.H.

1

Introduction

Lowell Milken

Although human potential and human nature have surely not changed over the past decade, the changes in the world around us have been seismic. The collapse of one of the defining political institutions of the past century has created worldwide repercussions. But its effect is a mere rumbling in our lives compared with that coming from the collapse of the basic institutions that for so long upheld this country's community structure and whose leadership animated it. These are the pillars of the family, the school, the place of worship, and the agencies of health care and social welfare. When institutions as fundamental as these are undermined and fail to fulfill their purpose, society sustains losses on many fronts, none more devastating than that of trust. And more often than not, trust eroded is trust foregone.

For more than a decade, the Foundations of the Milken Families have been working to help people help themselves and those around them lead satisfying and productive lives. This mission has been carried out in many respects by anticipating and answering needs arising from the absence or inadequacy of the basic caregiving institutions of the four areas on which we focus: education, community service, health care and medical research, and human welfare. Understanding the potential and connectedness of our basic caregiving institutions—the ways they can improve people's lives and the need for developing them—has been a *critical element* in our Foundations' evolution. We believe it is not only meaningless, for example, but hypocritical for society to talk about the well-being of children if we fail to address the fragmentation of the family, to enjoin youngsters to finish school if we fail to offer jobs to high school graduates, to invoke respect for human dignity if we turn away from the homeless and the hungry, or to decry the crisis in education if we fail to support the professionals who are its lifeblood.

Every day the Foundations of the Milken Families work with people left behind by once-supportive, once-protective institutions, and we see that often their problems feed into each other and take on a spiraling life of their own. A life of poverty, for instance, usually includes inadequate housing, poor nutrition, if not outright hunger, and human beings who are alone and broken. Broken people tend to hurt each other, if only through neglect, and the consequences of neglect for children are devastating. No statistic can begin to convey the trauma and need that propel children and teenagers into the hell of drugs for escape, into the arms of an uncaring stranger for affection, and, soon after, into rehab programs, abortion clinics, and halfway houses.

Scenes of destitution are hardly confined to inner-city settings. The vast majority of poor children are white and come from working families (Hewlitt, 1991). The child poverty rate in rural America is higher than in the nation as a whole, and one-fourth of poor children in the United States live in rural areas (Children's Defense Fund, 1991).

Although the weight of these problems bears down hard on all the areas in which we work, the needs behind them converge most forcefully in the school—which is just one reason education is our primary area of activity. Indeed, that concerns as diverse as basic health care, emergency health care, nutrition, parental neglect, and spiritual guidance should have become the direct responsibility of educators indicates a sea of change in the working of our schools and in the way society construes schools.

Why *has* the school become the axis of human and social service delivery? In our view, there are three fundamental reasons. First, the school is, in the most literal sense, a vital institution, existing for the well-being of *children*. Second, the school system, however frustrated and freighted, is firmly established. And third, and most important, the school continues to be both a repository and a generator of trust. And *this* is attributable to the impact of *educators*. From the inner city through the suburban periphery to rural settings of every description, it is the educator who is on the front lines ministering to the needs of our youth. A generation of children is being entrusted to our teachers and principals—apparently to be educated, but, increasingly, to be saved.

Fortunately, children are vessels of great faith and compassion. They are also our legacy and our hope. But there is little use in saying that children are our hope if we fail to acknowledge that, even more crucially, *we are theirs*. Because we are dedicated to fulfilling that hope, the first commitment of the Foundations of the Milken Families is to the field of education; the future, quite simply, *belongs* to the educated. And because it is the responsibility of every generation to safeguard the future of the next, we commit the largest part of our resources to programs in education, programs that respond to students imaginatively, engage parents fully, and support and celebrate educators substantially and publicly.

Specifically, our primary and ongoing aim is to establish a covenant with the educator. As professionals, educators are second to none in their exponential impact on society. As role models, they are second only to parents. In recognition of their importance and impact, in the early 1980s the Milken Family Foundation conceived an educator award program to focus on the needs and resources of educators, to help elevate the status of the profession, and to provide strong motivation for creative and talented young men and women to become educators themselves. Formally initiated in California in 1987, the program has since expanded to 20 states in every region of the country as the Milken Family Foundation National Educator Award program.

Over the past several years, the Awards have had a measurable impact, we believe, in the lives of both educators and children. It is deeply encouraging to hear from so many recipients about the effects the Awards have had on their careers, their families, their colleagues, and especially their students.

Our faith in the multiplier effect of the educator's influence has been borne out not only by the Award recipients' work with their students and colleagues but also by the recipients' effects upon each other. This has been demonstrated annually at the Milken Family Foundation National Educator Awards Retreat. This three-day conference, held each spring in Los Angeles, has two essential purposes: to *further the professional development* of past and present Award recipients by bringing them together with other distinguished educators from throughout the country to address issues that particularly bear on the practitioner; and to *celebrate publicly the professional achievement* of the current year's recipients with the $25,000 attached to each of the Awards, which numbered 312 as of the 1992 Retreat. The Retreat has explored such specialized topics as tracking in schools (1989) and appropriate test preparation practices (1990) as well as such global issues as how we can cultivate the graduates we want (1991). In 1993, we examine the urgent and far-reaching issue of family and community involvement in education. The present volume treats the substance of the 1992 Milken Family Foundation National Educator Awards Retreat, the topic of which, "How to Improve Schools," stimulated three days of spirited and, we believe, constructive debate.

Highlights of the Retreat presented in this volume include economist Dr. Lewis Solmon's presentation. President of the Milken Institute for

Job & Capital Formation, Dr. Solmon profiles our newest and only non-grant-making foundation—a think tank dedicated to improving the climate for job creation and capital formation. Dr. Solmon also offers a detailed analysis of the vital links between education and the economy.

Delivering the first of the Retreat's two keynote addresses, Dr. Chester Finn, a former assistant secretary of education and professor of education and public policy at Vanderbilt University, discusses possible directions for education reform in the context of "a vast transformation of the very meaning of education." Citing seven unsolved problems that bedevil reform efforts, Dr. Finn considers such issues as the "retail complacency" exhibited in most quarters even in the face of crisis and the imperative that schools be relieved of responsibilities beyond their purview. He also offers his "10 essential requisites of a properly reformed education system."

Dr. Henry Levin, director of Stanford University's Center for Educational Research and professor of education and affiliated professor of economics at that university, presents the second keynote address. Starting from the belief that all children can learn, Dr. Levin contends that children at risk of failure do better in school when more—not less—is expected of them. The accelerated approach, designed by Dr. Levin's Stanford Accelerated Schools Project, holds that "at-risk students must learn at a faster rate than more privileged students," and that "an enrichment strategy is called for, rather than a remedial one." By instilling "unity of purpose" within the school hierarchy, encouraging "school-site empowerment," and building on the strengths of all involved, Dr. Levin creates a compelling model of education reform.

Chapters presenting the working part of the Retreat include a galvanizing contribution by Linda Darling-Hammond, who takes on the topic of how innovative educators can create innovative schools. Dr. Darling-Hammond, professor of education at Teachers College of Columbia University, is also co-director of the National Center for Restructuring Education, Schools, and Teaching.

If one clear consensus emerged from the 1992 Retreat, it is that it will take an immense and sustained effort on many fronts to effect real, systemic improvement in education and to produce a preponderance of students and graduates who are purposeful and competent. The good news is that a serious effort to improve education has been joined in schools all across the country, in the hundreds of classrooms and principals' offices where Milken Family Foundation National Educator Award recipients—and the many other outstanding educators they represent—are teaching, awakening, and guiding students toward the fullness of their potential.

Valerie Mills, a 1990 Milken Family Foundation National Educator Award recipient and a high school mathematics teacher from Ypsilanti, Michigan, provides an insightful synthesis of fellow Award recipients' responses to the Finn and Levin presentations. Culled from the proceedings of 20 workshops following the keynote talks, Ms. Mills's account touches on issues as diverse as the overarching need for schools to have a vision, the essential role of parents in children's education, standard setting, criteria measuring, educator reward systems, and the increasingly urgent question of how schools and educators are to respond to the full scope of noneducation demands placed on them.

Dr. Linton Deck, director of education and non-profit sector applications for the Center for Creative Leadership, addresses creative leadership in education in a chapter on the practitioner with Gordon Ambach, executive director of the Council of Chief State School Officers.

Since its establishment, the Milken Family Foundation National Educator Award program has identified and honored a group of men and women extraordinary not only for their talent and dedication but also for their sheer human diversity. As this assembly is fast becoming a nationwide network with great synergistic potential, in January 1992 the Milken Foundation undertook a survey of Award recipients to obtain a fuller understanding of how various details of background, upbringing, education, and values come together to form a superlative educator. We were also interested in learning about the recipients' perceptions of the impact of the recognition and the major monetary award it carries with it. The findings of that survey are summarized by Dr. Cheryl Fagnano in the concluding chapter of this volume.

Decades of involvement and inquiry and more than 10 years of formal service have confirmed our instinctive belief that education does more than any other profession to realize human potential. But releasing that potential and securely transporting our youth from this century to the next cannot and should not depend on one profession alone. Safeguarding our future requires a radical rethinking of our communities, their needs, and their resources; it requires the rebuilding and the creation of the caregiving institutions that give them stability; it demands a call to leadership among the people who give them their force; and it demands firm and ongoing support *by* those institutions for the men and women who are creating programs and working to assure the well-being of others.

As our mission makes clear, we believe that "A wealth of human potential is represented by individual men and women of vision and purpose, each of whom can be, given resources and support, a dynamic force for change." As the Foundations of the Milken Families move into our second decade, we have expanded this mission to include a commitment to both reviving existing institutions and developing new ones in order to provide the catalytic, structural support that even the most creative individuals need to bring about transformative change. To carry out such change—and to anticipate new needs effectively—requires an unqualified and collective commitment from all sectors: government, business, and nonprofit. It also requires the full participation of parents, for the family is and will always be our most important caregiving institution.

The mission is urgent, and the climate for change exists. One of the world's last empires has expired, and hundreds of millions of lives have been transformed overnight by the possibilities—however complex and demanding—of freedom. That freedom—to think for ourselves, to express our ideas, and to make life better for our own sake and the sake of those around us—has long been ours in this country. We are also endowed with the resources, particularly the human resources, that give that freedom its meaning.

The achievements of the people with whom we have had the privilege of working are *proof*—powerful and positive—that we have the resources we need to make our communities supportive, our institutions vibrant, and our individual lives satisfying and productive. What we need now is the *determination* to work together. Only then will we have the potential to make a profound difference in assuring human well-being.

2

The Economic Context of Education Reform

Lewis C. Solmon

Though the challenges facing education have most certainly grown over the years, they are being met, to a large degree, by people such as the participants in this Retreat, men and women who represent the pinnacle of the most demanding and the most noble of all professions. It is no secret that education at all levels in this country is in crisis. In fact, it faces many crises: It is suffering from inappropriate use of its resources, it has structural problems, it has problems with output, and problems with personnel. It is being shaken by the deterioration of complementary and fundamental institutions, such as the family, and, perhaps worst of all, it is struggling with an identity crisis of the first order.

But, for all of that, there is still reason for hope. In recent years, we have seen more people, better people, and people who are ever more dynamic entering the profession. And as we begin new efforts in school reform, it is likely that we will see improvements in student achievement. Indeed, if we think about all the new responsibilities being given to our schools without commensurate new funding, we may well conclude that K-12 education has not been doing as bad a job as some have charged over the past few years.

Nor should we lose sight of the fact that the predicament of education, with all its challenges and with all the responses to those challenges, is not unlike that of other sectors. Similarly, the problems of and solutions to the crisis in education are closely linked to the solutions in those other sectors.

The links between education and the economy, for example, are close and strong. A strong, growing economy promotes a strong educational system, just as a strong educational system and a well-educated population are the sine qua non of a growing economy. True, more and better schooling confers a wide variety of benefits both on the individual and on society at large, but it is also true that a major promise of education and the system upholding it for generations has been that more education leads to better jobs and a lifetime of higher earnings. If, however, the economy is stagnant, and if businesses and industries are declining and closing down rather than growing and being created, that fundamental promise—that education leads to prosperity—is hollow.

The Milken Institute for Job & Capital Formation has been established to have a positive impact on job creation, on capital formation, on business development, and on economic growth in the United States. The Institute conducts and supports research and discourse on the levers of American economic growth. Occasionally, it also sponsors collaborative programs—usually pilot projects—designed to put into action ideas generated by the Institute and aimed at developing the economies of local communities.

A notable example of this sort of undertaking can be seen in the University Community Outreach Project (UCOP), which matches the strengths and human resources of urban universities with the economic and educational development needs of their local communities. On the basis of the success at our four UCOP sites, we may well expand the program to other locales as well as develop similar enterprises with different constituencies.

Although the Institute does a certain amount of programming for economic development in communities, our primary impact flows from research, policy analysis, conferences, and publications. We are, in short, a research institute—a policy institute, a think tank.

Our research program is well under way, both in-house and at leading universities around the country. In October 1992 we plan to hold a conference titled "Economic Policy, Financial Markets, and Economic Growth," which will convene a Who's Who of financial economists to discuss policies intended to stimulate long-term economic growth, job creation, and capital formation. We are also publishing a quarterly Institute newsletter, which features diverse views on pressing issues related to the growth of the American economy.

The Institute occupies a special niche among the recent proliferation of think tanks. Our approach is neither as narrow as that of those who focus on a single issue, such as energy or taxation, nor as broad as that of those who cover the entire waterfront—from defense policy to health care. We are studying a focused, cohesive set of issues.

Our inquiries deal with such topics as where new jobs will come from and how to expand job opportunities; the organization and structure of corporations; the capital structures of American corporations and their access to financial capital; the strength of our financial institutions; monetary and fiscal policy; federal, state, and local regulatory policy; tax policy; the role of individual leaders and entrepreneurs; the quality of education and access to it; the need for research support, technology, and innovation; and America's role in the international economic community—all of which are factors influencing economic growth and job creation.

The Institute is not beholden to any point of view, nor is our stance either liberal or conservative by definition. It automatically hews neither to the Democratic nor to the Republican position. Our basic hypothesis, rather, is that the American economic system can work, and our chief aim is to identify policies that will make it work optimally. The generosity and vision of the Milken families enable us to analyze policies and to carry out projects without being subject to changing trends and tastes or to the vagaries of various funding agencies.

As we have traveled and talked with leading economists and policy analysts around the country, the response to our mission has been very favorable: "Boy, do we need you!" We hear that over and over. And indeed, one need only read the daily newspapers to see how relevant and necessary our enterprise is. Let's consider, for a moment, the proposals offered by the so-called experts for stimulating the economy, creating jobs, and encouraging capital formation. To begin with, everyone knows exactly what should be done. Everyone also has a different opinion on what should be done. Here is a small sample of the ideas emanating from the ongoing debate over U.S. economic growth.

One major school of thought perceives salvation in the tax code. Cut personal income taxes either on the rich or on the middle class. Cut the capital gains tax. Give people bigger personal exemptions. Substitute a tax credit for the personal exemption. Cut marginal tax rates for everybody. Cut marginal tax rates for some and raise them for others, such as the rich. Cut taxes on labor income. Cut taxes on capital income. Cut taxes temporarily. Cut taxes permanently. Eliminate the home mortgage interest deduction. Expand the home mortgage interest deduction. Encourage savings. Encourage consumer spending. Others suggest a cut in the corporate income tax.

Fiscal policy yields the same diversity of opinion. Cut government spending. Increase government spending on (choose one of you're a Republican, three if you're a Democrat) research/infrastructure/education/health/jobs. Cut middle-class entitlements. Cut welfare. Raise welfare. Balance the budget. Prime the government pump more. Transfer responsibility to states and localities. Take the burden off states and localities. Create more public service jobs. Cut government employment and bureaucracy.

And what about our related friends, monetary policy and regulation of financial markets? Keep money tight. Loosen it up. Let the market allocate capital. Have the bank examiners apply tighter standards. Have the bank examiners loosen their standards. Get rid of deposit insurance. Strengthen deposit insurance. Speed up RTC (Resolution Trust Company) and FDIC shutdowns of weak institutions. Slow down RTC and FDIC shutdowns of weak institutions. Dismantle the RTC altogether.

Nor can we forget the business sector or foreign trade. Encourage business investment. Encourage reduction of business debt. Discourage use of high-yield bonds. Encourage innovation in financial markets. Enforce antitrust. Encourage business cooperation on R&D. Let businesses downsize for efficiency. Promote worker loyalty by eliminating layoffs. Automate. Use workers more efficiently.

Cut oil imports. Buy oil where it's cheapest. Defend free trade. Retaliate against "unfair" trade or "dumping." Sign a North American free trade agreement. Urge consumers to "buy American." Cut immigration and save American jobs. Encourage immigration and reduce labor costs. Make the dollar stronger. Encourage foreign investment in the United States. Don't let foreigners buy up the country.

Well, there you have it. Now that we know all the solutions, let us step back and ask what the problems are. For all the talk about current crises, the fact is that many of these problems are short-term. A major focus of our Institute will be on long-term issues facing the American economy.

The measure of our economic well-being most closely examined in recent months has been the unemployment rate. After peaking in 1982 during the Reagan recession at 9.7 percent, unemployment declined steadily during the 1980s. Even during the current or recently ended recession (depending upon which political party you believe), we have not returned to the unemployment levels of earlier recessions. At the end of 1991 the unemployment rate was 7.1 percent, and things have gotten somewhat worse since then.

Of course, the unemployment statistics deal only with people looking for jobs who cannot find them. If we add to the unemployed those people who have dropped out of the labor market because they have given up on finding jobs, the jobless figures are much worse. In that case we have 10 million people in this country who want jobs and cannot find them.

Moreover, there have been charges recently (and data to support them) that the U.S. Department of Labor (1992) estimates of unemployment may be understated by as much as 2 million nationally, with at least half of this shortfall occurring in a few major industrial states, such as California and New York.

What useful insights can be derived from our current unemployment problem? First, much of the unemployment has come from cutbacks in large, high-profile companies. These cutbacks are not merely cyclical;

rather they are the result of various types of permanent restructuring. Our nation's largest companies are reducing their staffs permanently; they are automating, or they are merging. It is getting so bad that the three largest car manufacturers in the United States may soon be Mattel, Tonka, and Matchbox.

Sadly, workers being dropped often have little prospect of being rehired once the recession ends. Between 1979 and 1990, employment in the Fortune 1,000 manufacturing and service firms fell by 2.3 million (*Fortune*, 1981a, 1981b, 1991a, 1991b).

Dan Lacey (1992), editor of *Workplace Trends*, estimates that in 1991, publicly held U.S. corporations announced a total of 556,092 permanent staff cuts. This does not include temporary workforce layoffs to trim inventories or production. Lacey estimates that an equal number of permanent cuts that have not received national press coverage are omitted from his figure.

During the steady decline in employment in large firms during the 1980s, the drop was more than offset by increased hiring in smaller firms. New firms were being created and existing firms with innovative goods and services flourished and grew. Smaller firms accounted for more than 100 percent of total employment growth in the 1980s. The result was an overall growth in employment in goods and services production of more than 20 million people, despite the loss of more than 2 million jobs in Fortune 1,000 companies (*Employment and Earnings*, 1992; *Fortune*, 1981a, 1981b, 1991a, 1991b).

Today, two out of every three new jobs in the United States are created by small and medium-sized businesses (Birch, 1987). Given that the majority of Americans work in small enterprises, the importance of this sector for employment and real economic growth cannot be overstated.

The latest data show that new business starts are still 12 percent below their peak of December 1986, when 66,000 new businesses were incorporated (*Monthly Business Failures*, 1991a). Another survey shows that, after rebounding in early 1991, small business optimism has fallen for three consecutive quarters. Unless this important sector is given new incentives, weak job creation, income, and consumer confidence will dampen prospects for near-term economic recovery.

Since early 1990, the rise in business failures has dramatically outpaced the rate of new business incorporation. According to Dunn & Bradstreet, between October 1990 and October 1991 new business incorporations increased 2.2 percent, but business failures rose 39.6 percent (*Monthly Business Failures*, 1991b).

The near-term employment outlook for small businesses remains rather dim. In a sample of nearly 2,300 small firms that employ about half of the private nonfarm workforce, the National Federation of Independent

Business found that only 13 percent plan to increase employment in the next six months (*Quarterly Economic Report on Small Business*, 1991). This suggests it may be some time before nonfarm payrolls post the sizable gains necessary to confirm recovery. As long as job creation is weak and unemployment claims are high, consumer confidence will be subdued and incomes will remain flat.

Although 44 percent of small firms expect business conditions to improve, only 10 percent feel now is a good time to expand. What, then, is holding back the small business sector? The main constraints to small business expansion appear to be poor fiscal and regulatory policies.

Each year since 1988, firms have cited rising tax and regulatory costs as their two biggest problems. Over the same period, the Fed succeeded in lowering inflation from 5 percent to 2 percent, and interest rates from more than 9 percent to 7.5 percent; as a result, less than 10 percent of the firms surveyed by the National Federation of Independent Business indicated interest rates were a main concern. Less than 5 percent cited inflation as their biggest problem (*Quarterly Economic Report on Small Business*, 1991).

Many of the forces behind the boom of the 1980s have been vitally curtailed. In particular, access to capital has been drastically reduced by new regulations imposed on banks, savings and loan institutions, and securities markets. High-yield financing, for example, which provided more than $45 billion to entrepreneurs in 1986, provided only $2.7 billion in 1990 (Dunn, 1992).

During the 1980s, some large banks made unwise decisions—loaning money to investors who overbuilt real estate, to problematic ventures in foreign countries, and to risky ventures at home. Thus, these banks fell upon hard times, and the response of the government was to tighten and intensify its regulatory activities. A by-product of these efforts was that small and medium-sized businesses found it increasingly difficult to obtain financing, and so potential new job opportunities were reduced.

As the economy, because of increased regulation of financial institutions and capital markets, shifts away from the entrepreneurial activities that would have resulted from greater access to capital, many of today's unemployed despair of future prospects. And many of these people used to hold jobs that had seemed secure, recession-proof. This has been a recession not only of workers in general, but of white-collar professionals and the educated in particular. So current unemployment should not be blamed entirely on lack of talent or energy among the unemployed. There is something more fundamental at issue. Understanding the causes of the recent destruction of jobs and analyzing policies to help reverse the trend are central aims of the Milken Institute's research program.

Another subject of much debate in recent months has been the productivity of American workers. Worker productivity grew by 2.6 percent in 1976, and by 2.4 percent in 1983, but remained relatively flat between 1989 and 1991 (Council of Economic Advisers, 1992). There are many technical problems with published measures of labor productivity that need not be discussed here. Let us consider, however, a few obvious factors affecting productivity.

First is the K-12 educational system. Productivity growth will be hampered if the quality of education declines. Although test scores certainly do not tell the whole story (and though they have improved somewhat in recent years), they provide an important indication of just how badly many of our children are doing, particularly when compared with their peers in other advanced countries. The Milken Family Foundation is investing very substantial resources and significant effort in helping to rectify some of the essential problems of K-12 schooling.

Second, the productivity of any factor of production, such as labor, rises when the quantity or quality of complementary factors, such as machines and equipment or infrastructure, increases. Over the past 20 years, the real tax rate on capital has risen significantly, and this, along with increasingly restrictive regulations in financial markets, has both diminished and distorted capital investment. The short-term, self-interested, pork-barrel mentality of many politicians has, moreover, encouraged the inefficient use of public resources, even as planning continues for such federally funded projects as a Lawrence Welk Museum.

Finally, social variables also affect labor productivity. As our nation gets older, as the cost of health care rises, as traditional family units splinter and in many communities cease to exist, labor productivity declines. The share of families headed by single women grew from 13.5 percent in 1975 to 17.7 percent in 1990. A great proportion of these single women are young and never married rather than widowed or divorced, as in the past (U.S. Bureau of the Census, 1992). The hard-core health and social welfare problems implicit in these trends are key concerns of the Foundations of the Milken Families, and the Foundations' demonstrable impact in these areas is cause for real hope.

Still, as education suffers in many places, and as families and communities disintegrate, so does worker productivity. And when workers produce less, employers are tempted to automate, to hire fewer people, and to move production to places where workers produce more or will work for less. So once again we see fewer jobs and more people in despair. Median family income is not much different in real terms today from its 1978 or 1979 level. It was lower during the recession of the early 1980s, but it rose throughout the rest of the decade until it fell once again in 1990 (U.S. Bureau of the Census, 1992).

Certainly the percentage of families headed by single women has risen steadily during the past decade. On the other hand, many families have attempted to maintain their living standards by having both parents work. The effects of both of these trends on traditional family structure and values and on the well-being of children are troubling. Even traditional families do not think that the future will be better than the present. There is simply less optimism than there was a few years ago.

It is unclear now whether there are proportionally more poor people than in the past. There will always be a bottom third of the income distribution, but the poor are more visible today owing to an increase in homelessness during the 1980s despite increased welfare spending. This increased dislocation has resulted from new zoning laws that enabled the conversion of single-room occupancy hotels into upscale tourist accommodations and urban renewal projects that, while revitalizing downtown areas, have driven up rents and reduced housing for the poor. Increased homelessness is also attributable to rent control laws, to economic changes that eliminated unskilled jobs that paid enough for workers to support their families, and the states' deinstitutionalization of the mentally ill and reduced funding of local community health programs.

The increasingly global nature of economic activity and competition increases wealth on average, but it also expands income distribution because the ratio of skilled/educated workers to unskilled/less educated workers in the United States is higher than that ratio for the world economy (Reich, 1991). Worldwide competition thus raises the wages of the educated relative to those of the uneducated in the United States, with the result that the number and wealth of the educated have grown, and the gap between rich and poor has widened.

Still, the proportion of families in the top income categories has risen, and the proportion in lower income categories has fallen (Reynolds, 1992). Most are better off, even though the gap between rich and poor has widened. Nevertheless, those in the lowest income categories still warrant our concern. It is difficult to take comfort in the fact that the median family income of the lowest quintile in our nation has risen since 1982 if we consider that (1) the 16 percent increase has been from $8,600 in 1982 to $9,941 in 1989, (2) family income fell again between 1989 and 1990, and (3) the growth for the highest quintile was from $79,266 in 1982 to $94,404 in 1990, or 19 percent. This is underlined when we see the suffering experienced by so many poor families today (Reynolds, 1992).

Issues such as these are the focus of the Milken Institute for Job & Capital Formation. What are the long-term prospects for job creation in the United States, for example? Where will the jobs be, and how can they be developed? How can access to capital be enhanced for the creative entrepreneurs who have ideas for enterprises that create jobs? How can we get our economy moving again—for the long haul?

What are the proper roles for education, social programs, government regulation, trade policy, monetary policy, government spending and taxing? In the long run, the solutions to these problems will not be found in such slogans as "Buy American," any more than President Ford succeeded with his "WIN" (Whip Inflation Now) buttons.

There was a significant lesson in the 1980s economy, which boomed while the costs of federal regulation declined. In the past three years, we have seen growth in regulation once again. We know what has happened to the economy in the past couple of years, and we are beginning again to see government spending rise as a share of GNP as well.

We need fundamental, dispassionate analysis of our economy, and the Milken Institute is here to provide it. We need to look at the kinds of issues touched upon here not only because of the special nature of this recession, but also because of our concern for the effects on people of the long-term health of the American economy. We must study these issues not only because we are all likely to know people who have lost their jobs this time around, not only because television has made us more aware than ever of homelessness and despair, but fundamentally because we are concerned with our children's well-being and with the well-being of their children and their children's children.

It is axiomatic that job creation and capital formation are inextricably linked with the soundness of our education system. We believe that the efforts of the Milken Institute for Job & Capital Formation, joined with the commitment and talent of teachers and principals such as those who have received the Milken Family Foundation National Educator Award, are destined to have a positive and enduring impact on the essential well-being of the American people.

3

Whither Education Reform?

Chester E. Finn, Jr.

From one source after another, for the past decade we have been receiving evidence that American education, taken as a whole, is doing a mediocre job, one that ill serves this country and our children. What is most alarming is that after a sustained period of valiant reform effort—and no small investment of resources—we have so little to show for our labors and our money.

For the United States as a whole, per student expenditures for public education increased an average of 35 percent in real dollars (i.e., after allowing for inflation) during the past 10 years. The figures vary by region, of course, but in the country as a whole we spent some $6,300 per pupil during the 1992–93 school year. In 1982–83, when *A Nation at Risk* (National Commission on Excellence in Education, 1983) was issued, the per pupil figure was $3,200 (National Center for Education Statistics, 1992).

Besides spending more on education, we have been trying conscientiously to make the enterprise more effective. Yet test scores remain flat. International comparisons continue to show us near the rear of the pack in most subjects; the latest figures rank our students' performance in the same range as Slovenia in science and math (Lapointe et al., 1992). Remedial education is the fastest-growing activity on many college campuses. Employers say they still cannot find competent workers. The quality of our civic and political life keeps eroding.

To be sure, American education can also boast some remarkable accomplishments over the decades. We have done well at constructing a universal and flexible system in which just about everybody can have just about as much education as they want, pretty much whenever they want it. We have also done well in recent years at increasing access for minorities, immigrants, and the handicapped. We are pretty good at recognizing student differences and trying through the schools to respond to those differences. Ours is an adaptive and fairly forgiving system, in which it is never too late to try again.

We have greatly increased access to higher education, too, such that the United States is the only country in the history of the world where more than half the secondary school completers commence further studies (National Center for Education Statistics, 1992). (Although Germany, it may be noted, now outstrips us in the rate at which young adults *graduate* from universities.)

We have a lot to be pleased with. Our accomplishments, however, cannot mask the bad news, above all the weak intellectual skills and knowledge possessed by our average high school graduate, and the widening gap between those skills and knowledge and the levels required for the kinds of jobs being created in the United States today; the kinds of jobs we have to be able to fill with qualified individuals if we are to be economically strong, not to mention culturally vibrant, civically alert, and internationally secure.

The problem, however, is not with basic skills any longer. According to data from the National Assessment of Educational Progress (NAEP), just about everyone who sticks with formal education through high school graduation now acquires rudimentary literacy and numeracy (Educational Testing Service, 1991; Johnson, 1992). At these very modest levels, one can say that we have made it "back to the basics"—and that was worth doing. It is when we look at the levels we really think people *should* reach—and their capacity to solve the sorts of problems the world actually presents—that attainments plummet.

Consider, for example, the latest NAEP math results, taken from 1990. (The 1992 data will be available soon. I've had a peek. They're nothing to cheer about.) Though virtually all eighth graders were successfully handling math concepts of the kind commonly introduced by third grade (addition and subtraction of whole numbers, that sort of thing), barely three in five were functioning at the level we associate with the fifth-grade math curriculum: multiplication and division, problems with more than one step, and so on. And only about one in seven was succeeding with problems involving fractions, decimals, percentages, and simple algebra, the sorts of things introduced by seventh grade (Educational Testing Service, 1991).

There is similar news in grades 4 and 12 in math, and comparable results in other core subjects such as reading, writing, science, history, geography, civics, and economics. The issue is not whether these results have fallen from some earlier golden age—in many cases they are just flat. The point is that they are not good enough for the United States in the 1990s. Our schools are not producing new adult illiterates, but they are graduating an enormous number of people with mediocre skills and knowledge, and that, above all, is why the nation is still "at risk."

I am dwelling here on outcome gauges, and this is appropriate if one accepts a more general proposition: that the United States is in the midst of a vast transformation of the very meaning of education. For a long time we construed education in terms of intentions and efforts, plans and inputs, institutions, resources, and services. Now we're moving to redefine education in terms of how much people actually learn. One day we will say of a person, "He had no education," however long he may have spent in school, if in fact he has not learned. We will no longer accept the statement, "I taught it, but they didn't learn it." Instead, the education system of tomorrow will be outcomes driven and highly accountable for its results.

Yet it is precisely when viewed in those terms that our reform efforts to date have not borne much fruit. No, I'm not passing final judgment. American education is large, decentralized, ponderous, and slow to change. Kids still take 17 years to reach their seventeenth birthdays, and most need 12 or 13 of those years to pass through the schools. Some of the boldest reform plans are really just commencing. So there may be progress in the making that has not yet shown up in the outcomes data. We all hope so.

But I am gloomy. I believe that a number of problems beset our education reform efforts that we have not come anywhere near to solving—in some cases even to acknowledging. I review seven of these problems below.

The first we can term *retail complacency*. There is a good deal of evidence that people are not changing their actual behavior despite all the alarms of the past decade concerning the condition of American education. We can glimpse a form of widespread schizophrenia, in which people seem, on the one hand, to acknowledge that we have a grave national education problem but also seem, on the other hand, to be reasonably content with their own and their children's education and with their local schools. It is a way of saying, "The nation is at risk, but I'm okay." Following is some evidence.

First, the kids think they're doing well, even when they're not. Consider one of the recent international assessments (of math and science performance among 13-year-olds) that found American youngsters at or near the bottom. That part did not surprise me much. What staggered me were responses to the background question asking the children to agree or disagree with the statement "I am good at mathematics." It turned out that U.S. youngsters led the world in believing themselves to be good at math, while trailing the world in actual math performance (Educational Testing Service, 1991; Johnson, 1992).

The 1990 NAEP state-by-state math assessment asked a similar question. I am not sure how much to make of this, but children in the highest-scoring jurisdiction—namely, North Dakota—had the lowest opinion of their own math prowess, whereas those in the lowest-scoring jurisdiction, the District of Columbia, had the highest self-evaluations of their math skills (Committee for Economic Development, 1991). Various interpretations can be attached to these findings. One I would suggest is that we have been subjecting a lot of our kids, perhaps especially our minority youngsters, to a pernicious blend of low expectations and unjustified positive feedback, both designed to build their self-esteem but both guaranteed to discourage high achievement.

More data come from University of Michigan psychology professor Harold Stevenson (1987, 1992), who has spent years comparing the performance of elementary school students in the United States with that of youngsters in Taiwan, Japan, and China, and whose research includes surveys of the children's opinions and attitudes. American girls and boys, Stevenson has found, give themselves top ratings when probed about such characteristics as their own abilities, their educational attainment to date, and the performance they expect from themselves in the future. Asian children are far less certain that they will lead the pack. When first-graders were asked how well they believed they would do in mathematics next year, Stevenson (1992, p. 71) reports a much higher percentage of American students said they would be "among the best" than did Japanese or Chinese (Taipei) first-graders.

That's in elementary school. A recent survey conducted by Louis Harris and Associates (1992) suggests that high school graduates still show the effects of happiness pills. A total of 68 percent of them claimed that they had learned math well while in school, 66 percent said they had learned to write well, and 78 percent said they had learned to read well. Keep those numbers in mind—68, 66, and 78 percent—because when a group of employers was asked to rate the high school graduates they had recently hired along the same three dimensions, the favorable ratings were just 22, 12, and 30 percent. And when, in the same survey, a group of people working in higher education were asked to rate the high school graduates entering their colleges in the same three core skills, the favorable ratings were only 27, 18, and 33 percent.

This reality gap on the part of the young people has its analogue among their parents, too. On that same Harris survey, when asked how well the schools had prepared their children, among parents of those who went from high school into jobs, the favorable ratings for the three skills were 65, 56, and 67 percent. Among parents of those headed for college, the favorable ratings were 71, 77, and 82 percent—actually higher than the young people's own appraisal of their education.

The annual Gallup education poll also asks each parent to rate public schools in general and then the school attended by his or her eldest child (see Elam, 1992; Elam et al., 1991; Elam and Gallup, 1989). The pattern of responses has been pretty steady for the past decade. Parents display low opinions of schools in general but high opinions of their own children's schools. In 1992, they gave honors grades to schools in general just 19 percent of the time, whereas the schools attended by their eldest children received high marks from a remarkable 64 percent.

To my surprise, most teachers also say they think well of their schools. In the above-cited 1992 Harris poll, conducted for the Metropolitan Life Insurance Company, 93 percent of teachers surveyed said that their present schools were providing a good or excellent education to their students. That is not to say that teachers don't have complaints, criticisms, and faults to find, only that, when pressed, most of them think their schools are doing reasonably well as they are.

Much the same seems to be true of school administrators. Feistritzer, Quelle, and Bloom (1988) found in 1987 that 90 percent of superintendents and 88 percent of principals conferred A or B grades on their own schools, while less than 2 percent gave marks below C.

Local school board presidents are interesting hybrids. When asked to appraise public education as a whole, the scores they gave resembled those of the general populace: just 33 percent handed out "honors" grades. But, when asked to evaluate the schools of their *own* communities—institutions over which they presided as school board leaders—they echoed the teachers and administrators: 79 percent conferred A or B grades and none gave failing marks (Feistritzer et al., 1988).

Consider the implications for education reform: If the children think they are doing pretty well, if their parents think the children are doing well, if people think their local schools are doing well, and if the teachers and administrators in those schools agree with this appraisal, as do local policy makers, why should any community members feel inclined to alter their actual behavior, to demand different results from themselves or their children, or to agitate for significant changes in the schools their children attend?

Yet if the actual behavior of actual people does not actually change in millions of individual cases, there is no reason whatsoever to expect our national averages and aggregates to change. Our outcomes will remain flat. And that, I suggest, has at least something to do with why the results of our reform efforts to date have not been more positive. It also says to me that any education improvement plan that does not deal directly with the complacency problem is doomed to failure.

Why have we failed to get the message across at the "retail" level, when we have done a pretty good job of communicating it at the "wholesale" level? Several possible explanations suggest themselves, beginning with the well-known fact that Americans tend to be optimistic and somewhat self-satisfied. We think pretty well of ourselves. We don't much like bad news. We are inclined to believe that things tend to get better, not worse.

Our elected officials have let us down by not looking us in the eye and saying, "When I talk about educational meltdown, Mr. and Mrs. Abernathy, I'm talking about your Johnny and Janet and the school they attend, not about somebody else's children or the schools across town."

We also have what has become known as the "Lake Wobegon" effect of state and local testing programs—the phenomenon that finds virtually everyone to be performing above the "national average"—and we have a flood of upbeat press releases pouring from state and local education agencies, nearly always asserting that results are good and getting better (Cannell, 1989). These claims don't exactly lie so much as they overstate the favorable news. It has not been difficult to get away with this for decades, either, because one of the things we have never had in American education is some counterpart to what business calls an "independent audit." We have had nobody to tell education's shareholders whether the company is really profitable except for the company's own treasurer. The problem, obviously, is that even when the treasurer is completely honest, he or she labors under a definite incentive to paint the company's performance in the rosiest hues and to bury any contrary information in the fine print. That is why corporate shareholders demand independent reviews by certified accountants. But when it comes to our children's education we do nothing of the sort. Is it any wonder we get a lot more good news about how the schools are doing than is warranted by the reality of their performance?

A shortage of honest feedback is part of the explanation. But another possibility concerns me just as much. There is some evidence that young Americans are behaving *rationally* when they don't study very hard or learn much in school. Which brings me to the second of the seven unsolved problems of education reform. This one concerns the *dearth of real-world incentives* for strong academic performance.

Outside the yuppie elites clawing their way into places like Stanford and Yale, few Americans actually reap significant rewards from studying hard and learning a lot. Children ordinarily get promoted from one grade to the next regardless of how they do. Persistence will eventually yield a high school diploma, even if it connotes little more than rudimentary skills. Report cards along the way customarily consist of good news and cheery, upbeat comments, no matter the actual level of performance. High school graduates entering the workforce earn the same (for as long as eight years out of school, according to Cornell economist John Bishop, 1992), whether they take hard courses and earn high grades or enroll in gut classes and get C's. Employers merely ask whether they received a diploma; nobody ever looks at their transcripts, let alone compensates them differently according to their school records.

Higher education is just as unhelpful. Admission to most colleges and universities requires merely that one be able to walk through the door and write a check; only a tiny fraction of prospective college students seek admission to competitive campuses. For most people, entry to the nearby community college or state university is a sure thing, no matter what their high school records show. That's why it has been estimated that 95 percent of U.S. college students wouldn't be admitted anywhere else in the world.

Think about it. If we don't differentially reward high achievers—or penalize low performers—why should youngsters study hard and learn a lot, particularly when they have so many enticing distractions and short-term gratifications? How are we going to have an impact on the thinking of a 16-year-old trying to decide on a Tuesday evening whether to stay home and work on his science lab report and history paper or to go out with his friends?

Teenagers, in their own sometimes-crude way, are rational beings who go through this kind of calculation all the time. Is there any real payoff visible to them for making what you and I might think of as the right decision? If there isn't—if they feel no powerful, tangible, and reasonably immediate real-world incentives for educational success—I'm not sure we'll have much of it. At least not much more than we already have. Remember, most teenagers, and their parents, think they're doing okay in school already. So, in the main, do their teachers and principals.

The third unsolved problem arises from the truism that *people tend to learn only what they study*. Yet no state requires all its youngsters to take the full array of academic high school courses that the National Commission on Excellence in Education (1983) termed the "new basics." Because these subjects are not required, in a great many instances they are not taken. Because they aren't studied, they aren't learned.

Course taking has improved in recent years, at least for college bound students, but it is still pretty weak. In the high school graduating class of 1987, for example, only 35 percent of students had taken the combination of algebra I, algebra II, and geometry. Just 39 percent had taken both U.S. and world history. Only 17 percent had taken the combination of biology, chemistry, and physics (National Center for Education Statistics, 1992). And these were graduates, not dropouts. Among minority students, the academic course-taking patterns were skimpier still. We have a huge distance to go on this front. To some extent, we are flagellating ourselves because our children haven't learned things that, in reality, many of them have never even been exposed to.

The fourth problem is based on another truism, namely, that *people learn things in rough proportion to the amount of time they spend studying.* Yet the time factor has barely been touched in the course of our reform efforts. As a result, American youngsters spend less time engaged in academic learning than just about anyone else in the industrial world. We have shorter school days and years than most countries; our children do far less homework. We are tied for first place in television watching. Our kids are more apt (at the secondary level) to spend their after-school hours working at jobs than studying. Is it any wonder that they wind up knowing less than their age-mates in other lands? They *study* less. I suspect that reform schemes that fail to deal with the time factor cannot make much difference in the outcomes of American education.

The fifth problem is that, until awfully recently, *we have not been clear about our goals,* about what adequately educated young Americans would actually look like if we were producing them. The governors and President Bush began to correct this situation with the six big (and to my eye commendable) national education goals that they set forth in early 1990. But although a number of states and localities signed on to the America 2000 strategy for reaching these goals, we have a long way to go before this idea is internalized in the priorities of students, parents, and educators. A 1992 Gallup survey indicates that about three-fourths of Americans are not yet even acquainted with these goals (Elam, 1992). This is not a trivial matter. Only when people can describe the results they seek do they have much of a chance of attaining them. As Vermont's education commissioner says, any road looks like the right one if you don't have a destination in mind.

Sixth, it isn't just that we haven't known where we are heading. *We also have not known enough about the progress we are making.* Our information feedback and accountability systems are wholly inadequate for the task at hand. It is awfully hard to get accurate, intelligible, and trustworthy information about how well our children are learning and our schools are performing. We really need such information at six different levels: the individual youngster, the classroom, the school building, the local school system, the state, and the entire nation. We have pretty decent national information now, but the closer we get to real kids and real schools the more difficult good information is to obtain. For better or worse, people tend to take most seriously those things that are measured and reported. Student learning outcomes at these six levels have not been satisfactorily measured or reported.

Seventh, and finally, *we assign a great many things to schools that they cannot do,* and we do a weak job of enlisting others in their missions. The most alarming statistic in American education has nothing to do with test scores. It has to do with the tiny portion of children's lives for which the schools are responsible. This is easy to calculate. Put into the numerator 13 years times 180 days times 6 hours. In the denominator put 18 years times 365 days times 24 hours. The quotient is .09, or 9 percent. That's assuming full-day kindergarten and perfect school attendance. Only 9 percent of a young person's life, during his or her first 18 years on earth, is spent in school; 91 percent is spent elsewhere.

Think about the relative amounts of leverage. Think what is possible within 9 percent, especially if the other 91 percent isn't cooperating. When they are effective, within their 9 percent, schools can do a good job of imparting cognitive learning to children: history, chemistry, literature, and so on. But they are not powerful enough instruments that we should expect them also to prevent adolescent pregnancy, to redistribute income, to stop drug abuse, to halt the spread of AIDS, and more. Yet schools keep getting such additional duties thrust upon them, and they nearly always agree to try to carry them out. The sad fact is that alone they cannot solve these problems, and their willingness to try may let others off the hook. Spreading their efforts across too many fronts may also leave them effective on none.

The seven problems described above will, if left unsolved, bedevil our efforts to bring about nonincremental improvements in education performance. What to do differently? Everyone will have his or her own view. Here, very briefly, is my own vision of a dozen essential requisites of a properly reformed education system.

First, we must set clear outcome goals and standards, in which we spell out the skills and knowledge that we would like every young American, regardless of background, to reach by the threshold of adulthood. The country finally seems to be headed that way now, but years will pass before we get there. In the meantime, states and localities need to be clear about what *they* expect of their youngsters.

Second, once there are outcome standards in place, if they are high enough and if we are serious about virtually everyone meeting them, we must understand that many established practices of our education delivery system will have to change, beginning with how we explain to students just how much is expected of *them.* I would start by restating what we mean by compulsory school attendance, so that instead of having to do with birthdays, it has to do with learning something.

Third, we must recognize that getting essentially everybody up to a reasonable standard of intellectual attainment means that most young

Americans are going to have to spend a far larger fraction of their lives learning academic things. But the amount of time will not be the same for everyone. This portends large changes, both in the lifestyles of kids and families and in the ways we organize schools. Ultimately, it argues for breaking the ancient link between chronological age and grade level, probably doing away altogether with traditional grade structures in U.S. schools and moving youngsters along in relation to their actual performance.

Fourth, what I have said implies a fairly substantial core curriculum throughout entire school systems, states, perhaps the whole country. How much of the total school curriculum should be swept into this core is up for discussion. That there should be one is, it seems to me, self-evident.

Fifth, outside the common core, I believe there should be much variety among schools as to the rest of the curriculum, huge variation as to pedagogy, and great diversity concerning things such as school climate, schedule, the nature of the instructional setting, even the auspices under which the school is operated. And the surest way to get such diversity is plenty of school-site management. I'm convinced that site-level decisions can go quite a distance. In Chicago, they now include the power to hire and fire the principal. They could equally include the ability to contract with independent providers for all sorts of services, from lunch to security to specialized instruction.

Sixth, with schools encouraged to differ in many ways and to manage their own affairs, it stands to reason that students and their parents must be allowed to choose among them on the basis of those differences. I do not mean only those families fortunate enough to get into magnet schools or "gifted and talented" programs, rich enough to pay for private schooling, or desperate enough to give false addresses so their kids can go to particular schools. I mean every child and every family. In my view, it is a public policy sin to require students, against their will and their parents' wishes, to attend poor schools, that they wouldn't go near but for the compulsion when there are better ones not far away that they would prefer to attend, if only it were permitted.

Perhaps it is obvious, but let me add that choice also needs to include teachers and principals. *Everybody* in a school ought to want to be there.

Seventh, we have to work on external incentives as well as do all we can to make learning intrinsically rewarding. We need to enlist employers, college admissions officers, and others in a concerted effort to make it worthwhile for youngsters to study hard and learn a lot.

Eighth, for all this to work, there needs to be a crackerjack information feedback and accountability system, such that everyone can see how children, schools, districts, even whole states, are doing. Accountability can be thought of as a tripod, and all three of its legs need to be sturdy. The first is clear goals and standards. The second is reliable information as to whether and how well those goals are being achieved and as to standards being reached at each level of the enterprise where it matters. The third leg—the one that makes some people skittish—I call "consequences." When you have clear standards and your information feedback system signals that they're being met, good things should happen to the people and institutions that are achieving them. But when your data indicate that your standards are not being attained, something must change—some sort of intervention must occur—or we can be certain that the goals will continue not being achieved. Consequences thus come in two main varieties: the warm fuzzy kind that everyone likes, and the interventionist kind that produce changes in situations that in their present form are not succeeding.

Ninth, we need to leverage the 91 percent of children's lives spent outside schools. That has far-reaching implications. It starts, but doesn't end, with integrating parents far more directly and intimately into the work of formal education. This is commonly assumed to be the toughest nut to crack, and probably it is. Be clear that I am not referring only to what happens in school. I am talking about a community-wide strategy for achieving goals and for maximizing each child's potential. There is plenty of work to go around, but parents are the single most important influence in the 91 percent. We need them.

Tenth, we should be making sweeping changes in where we find and how we treat the professional personnel who work in our schools. That 9 percent is pretty precious stuff, and we don't dare squander any of it. I believe we should be seeking crackerjack principals and teachers in many places, not just among graduates of teacher colleges and administrator training programs. We should be differentiating their roles within the school and paying them according to those differences, as well as according to their effectiveness, the demand for their particular specialties, and the difficulty of their assignments. We should create incentives and rewards so that those who are good at what they do are properly thanked and compensated. But when someone doesn't cut it—well, let's never forget that we have an education system primarily for the benefit of its consumers, not its producers.

Eleventh, we should welcome the private sector into a larger role in the renewal of education, and I am not just talking about the Edison Project, a privately funded effort to build 1,000 private schools in the United States over the next decade. In the complex politics of American education, business leaders—and some elected officials—have been functioning as surrogates for the public's interest in education. That may sound curious—the private sector looking after the public interest—and I don't claim it always works that way. But I am certain that education needs a greater sense of enterprise, needs to be far more conscious of its bottom line, and needs a dose of the efficiencies, risk taking, incentive structures, and quality management techniques that the private sector, at its best, can bring to bear.

Twelfth, and finally, we should multiply the technologies of education—and I don't mean just computers. For far too long, we have organized our education efforts as if the only way for learning to occur is when one big person pours it into the ears of 27 or so small people seated at desks or tables in a room with four walls. This sometimes works well, but it is only one technology; there are hundreds more, some involving people and techniques, some involving various devices, materials, and software, some involving the ways in which we construct and organize schools, some involving all sorts of learning that can occur in other settings. Almost every other domain of modern life is more varied and more sophisticated today in terms of its technologies than is the education system. It is time—past time, really—to change that.

Well, that's twelve. Some of these ideas may seem radical, and in the present context of American education some of them are. But people say they are ready for radical changes in this domain. Let me cite a few more findings from the Gallup education surveys of the past two years (Elam, 1992; Elam et al., 1991):

- "Would you favor or oppose requiring the public schools in this community to conform to national achievement standards and goals?" 81 percent in favor, 12 percent opposed
- "Would you favor or oppose requiring the public schools in this community to use standardized national tests to measure the academic achievement of students?" 71 percent in favor, 20 percent opposed
- "Would you favor or oppose requiring the public schools in this community to use a standardized national curriculum?" 68 percent in favor, 24 percent opposed
- "If a public school in this community does not show progress toward the national goals within a reasonable time, would you favor or oppose not renewing the contracts of the principals and the teachers in that school?" 57 percent in favor, 32 percent opposed
- "In some nations, the government allots a certain amount of money for each child for his or her education. The parents can then send the child to any public, parochial, or private school they choose. This is called the 'voucher system.' Would you like to see such an idea adopted in this country?" 70 percent in favor, 27 percent opposed

- "How do you feel about extending the public school year in this community by 30 days, making the school year about 210 days or 10 months long? Do you favor or oppose this idea?" 55 percent in favor, 35 percent opposed
- "In most school districts, policy decisions and changes are made by the school board and its administrative staff. In a few districts, however, some of these decisions are made by councils composed of local public school teachers, principals, and parents. Which way would you prefer to have policy decisions made in the schools in this community—by the school board and its administrative staff or by a council of teachers, principals, and parents?" 79 percent prefer the councils of teachers, principals, and parents; 11 percent favor such decisions continuing to be made by the school board and its administrative staff

There is an underlying and obvious paradox that I would point out in conclusion. On the one hand, the data indicate widespread public receptivity to fundamental changes in the education system. On the other hand, the same surveys reveal widespread complacency about the performance of the education system as it is today. If people are complacent, they are not apt to want to change their ways, to reallocate their resources of money and time and energy, or to alter their lifestyles. I do not have this paradox figured out. It is possible that people want bigger changes from the education system than they are ready to make themselves. I believe we need big changes in the 91 percent as well as in the 9 percent. Indeed, I think both are essential if we are going to bring about non-incremental improvements in our results.

4

Beyond Remediation: Toward Acceleration for All Schools

Henry M. Levin

Current Practices for At-Risk Students

In the early 1980s, a rash of reports published by national commissions and other groups recommended national educational reforms to improve economic competitiveness. The most important of these was *A Nation at Risk,* produced by the National Commission on Excellence in Education (1983). Most of the recommendations in these reports addressed changes in secondary school programs for college-bound students, calling for more academic courses with more rigorous standards at that level. But at-risk students were not even meeting the "lower" standards that existed at that time, and they were dropping out in response to the academic demands. The reports said almost nothing about improving school effectiveness prior to high school to make it possible for at-risk students to meet both existing and higher standards.

Why were the reports of these commissions silent about at-risk students? In response to this question, I undertook a study on the demography, educational outcomes, and social consequences of this group of students (Levin, 1986), the results of which are summarized in the first section of this chapter. As an extension of that study, I began to explore the production of schooling for this group of children (Levin, 1988). Surprisingly, I found that the educational process in schools attended by these children was the *cause* of much of the problem rather than the solution.

In my research, I found that at-risk students started behind other students and got further behind the educational mainstream the longer they were in school. And this problem did not appear to stem from a lack of teacher dedication, a charge that had often been made. Paradoxically, it occurred because compensatory programs for the disadvantaged are designed to slow down the instruction of such students, on the assumption that they are less capable than others. Such students are placed into less demanding instructional settings—either by being pulled out of their regular classrooms or by adapting the regular classroom to their "needs"—to provide remedial or compensatory educational services. Although this approach appears to be both rational and compassionate, it has exactly the opposite consequences.

First, it reduces learning expectations on the parts of both the children and the educators assigned to teach them, and it stigmatizes both groups with a label of inferiority. Second, it slows down the learning process, so that at-risk students fall further and further behind the mainstream the longer they are in school. Third, the approach to remediation is to provide repetitive, low-level basic exercises through endless drill and practice. This educational experience is empty and joyless because it fails to incorporate a rich curriculum, student involvement and discourse, interesting applications of concepts, active problem solving, and learning activities that build on the strengths of the students and their backgrounds. Finally, this remedial approach does not draw sufficiently upon parental and community resources, nor does it provide for the participation of school-based educators to influence the programs they must implement.

I concluded from my research that an effective approach to educating the disadvantaged must be characterized by high expectations, deadlines by which children will be performing in the educational mainstream, stimulating instructional programs, planning by the educational staff who will offer the program, and the use of all available resources, including the parents of the students. The approach should incorporate a comprehensive set of strategies that mutually reinforce one another in creating an organizational push toward raising the achievement of students to the level we expect in the mainstream.

Accelerated Schools as a Solution

Accelerated schools were designed by the Stanford Accelerated Schools Project to bring at-risk students into the educational mainstream by the end of elementary school. Our premise was very basic: At-risk students must learn at a *faster* rate than more privileged students—not at a slower rate that allows them to fall further and further behind. An enrichment strategy is called for, rather than a remedial one.

It may seem strange to talk of acceleration for at-risk students. Educators usually reserve acceleration programs for their "gifted and talented" students, those who perform at the very top. Yet, one can't help wondering why we channel so much enrichment to help our best students get even better while we deliberately slow the pace of learning of children who lack educational advantages.

Acceleration works just as well for at-risk students. One recent study assigned at-risk students at random to remedial, average, and honors classes in seventh-grade mathematics. At the end of the year, the at-risk students in the honors class—which provided pre-algebra instruction—outshone those in the other two groups (Peterson, 1989). Knapp, Shield, and Turnbull (1992) evaluated instruction in 140 classrooms in 15 schools serving at-risk students. Over a school year they found that enriched instruction designed to create meaning and understanding was more effective in increasing knowledge of advanced skills and at least as effective in providing basic skills as was the more traditional remediation and basic skills approach. John Feldhusen (1992), a noted authority on gifted and talented education, has concluded:

> Schools should abandon efforts to identify "gifted students" as though they were a biologically distinct category of human beings and concentrate instead on: (1) searching for talent or strengths in all children, (2) searching for those who might have very high levels of talent or precocity in a "worthwhile area" of human endeavor, and (3) seeking to provide the best instruction possible to help youth develop their talents to the fullest. (p. 1)

Institutionalizing Change

Moving from an idea to institutional change is never an easy process, however. In order to develop a strategy for creating accelerated institutions, we found that we would have to make three major changes in U.S. schools, changes that were in deep conflict with current practices (Levin, 1988). These changes have deep economic roots in that they require the establishment of a clear objective function for the school (unity of purpose), the ability of those with de facto property rights to exercise those rights in behalf of children within a framework of incentives and accountability (school-site empowerment with responsibility), and the use of an appropriate technology of schooling that will deliver results (building on strengths).

Unity of Purpose

Most schools that educate at-risk students seem to lack any central purpose. In economic terms, they are firms without an objective function. Traditional schools are better understood as a composite of individuals and programs that seem largely disparate and piecemeal, with no central vision. Planning, implementation, and evaluation are typically done independently and by different groups. Teachers tend to see their responsibilities as extending no further than good practices in self-contained classrooms, and remedial specialists work in isolation from each other and the regular school program.

Acceleration requires the establishment and pursuit of a common vision that serves as a focal point for the efforts of parents, teachers, staff, and students. The vision of an accelerated school must focus on bringing children into the mainstream, where they can more fully benefit from school experiences and opportunities. The development of this vision requires the combined efforts and commitment of all parties involved. *Unity of purpose* refers to both a vision or dream of what the school can be and an action plan that will get the school there.

School-Site Empowerment

Existing schools for at-risk students are largely dominated by decisions made by entities that are far removed from the school site and classroom. Federal and state governments and central offices of school districts have established a compendium of rules, regulations, directives, policies, laws, guidelines, reporting requirements, and "approved" instructional materials that serve to stifle educational decisions and initiative at local school sites. It is little wonder that administrators, teachers, parents, and students tend to blame factors "beyond their control" for the poor educational outcomes of at-risk students. And compliance with these policies ensures failure, not success, as the historical record has shown.

An accelerated school requires on-site responsibility for the major decisions that will determine educational outcomes, through the establishment of a collective sense of efficacy and the skills and organization to undertake the changes that are necessary. If the school is to achieve its vision of educational success, administrators, teachers, other staff, parents, and students must participate in making informed decisions regarding school activities. Important areas of school-site decisions include some or all of the following: curriculum, instructional strategies, instructional materials, personnel, and allocation of resources inside the school. Such decision making requires active support from the district's central office in the form of information, technical assistance, staff development, and evaluation as well as an overall system of accountability in which the school is rewarded according to its performance.

Building on Strengths

Schools with large numbers of at-risk students tend to highlight the weaknesses of their students, staff, funding, administrative support, and so on as an explanation for poor performance. Particularly heavy emphasis is placed on the litany of what is wrong with at-risk students and their parents. But good pedagogy begins with the strengths and experiences of participants and builds on those strengths to overcome areas of weakness rather than dwelling on the weaknesses. This means that schools must shift from a technology of production that has shown consistent failure to one that has shown superior results.

Accelerated schools seek out the strengths of their students and other participants and use those strengths as a basis upon which to build their programs. In this respect, students are treated as gifted and talented; their strengths are identified and are then used as a basis for providing enrichment and acceleration. The strengths of at-risk students are often overlooked because they are not as obvious as those of middle-class students, but my research and that of my colleagues has shown that at-risk children bring assets that can be used to accelerate the learning process. These include interest and curiosity in oral and artistic expression, ability to learn through manipulation of appropriate learning materials and interesting applications, the capability to delve eagerly into intrinsically interesting tasks, and a capacity for learning to write prior to mastering reading skills.

The process of building on strengths is not just limited to students, however. Accelerated schools also build on the strengths of parents, teachers, and other school staff. Parents and teachers are largely underutilized resources in most schools. Parents, because they want their children to succeed, can be powerful allies if they are placed in productive roles and provided with the skills they need to work with their children. Teachers bring gifts of insight, intuition, and organizational acumen to the instructional process, gifts that are often untapped by the mechanical curricula that are so typical of remedial programs. Accelerated schools acknowledge the gifts of teachers and parents and build on those strengths in fulfilling their accelerated visions.

Combining the Principles

An accelerated school is not just a conventional school with new principles or special programs grafted onto it. It is a dynamic environment in which the entire school and its operations are transformed. The emphasis is on the school as a whole, rather than on a particular grade, curriculum, staff development approach, or other limited strategies. The goal is high academic achievement for *all* students.

The three principles of unity of purpose, site-based empowerment, and building on strengths are woven together in virtually all of the activities of the accelerated school. The school is governed by its staff, students, and parents, and priorities are pursued by task groups that follow a systematic inquiry process for problem solving, implementation, and evaluation.

Accelerated schools use a heavily language-based approach across all subjects, even mathematics, with an early introduction to writing and reading for meaning. The curricula reflect a sense of high expectations and ties to the students' cultures. Active learning experiences are provided through independent projects, problem solving, and applying learning to concrete situations. By applying academic concepts and skills to real-life problems and events, students see the usefulness of what they are learning.

The organization of accelerated schools allows for a broad range of participants and a collaborative approach in which students' families play a central role. Indeed, success depends on parents' working with staff and students, helping to make school decisions by participating in the decision-making bodies of the school.

Some Accelerated Results

The first two pilot accelerated schools were established in 1987 and have completed five years in operation. Complete transition from a traditional to an accelerated school takes about six years. Since 1987, approximately 140 additional schools have initiated the transition process; most of these are elementary schools, but there has been recent extension to middle schools. We have found that the transformation to an accelerated school can be done primarily by reallocating existing resources to free up time and make other provisions for staff development and accelerated school activities. To my knowledge, none of the schools has obtained additional funding that exceeds even one percent of its budget to pursue accelerated school activities. We who are involved in the Stanford Project believe that the basic transformation to and operation of an accelerated school can be done largely within existing resources. It should be noted that most of the other national educational reforms that have shown success have an additional cost of about $1,000 per student, in comparison with about $20 to $30 per student among accelerated schools.

Early results have been extremely promising. The Daniel Webster School in San Francisco enrolls a student body that is more than 90 percent minority and more than 80 percent on public assistance. It was one of the bottom elementary schools in San Francisco in 1987, with test scores in mathematics that were sixty-fifth out of 69 schools. By 1991, the mathematics scores had risen to twenty-third in San Francisco, among the top third of all schools. Students were performing above grade level in mathematics at every grade. Test score gains in all three areas that were tested—reading, language, and mathematics—were the highest among all schools in San Francisco. The Daniel Webster School was the only school in San Francisco in which both black and Spanish-surname students made more than a year of academic progress.

The Hollibrook Elementary School in Houston enrolls more than 1,000 students, many of them recently arrived immigrants from Central and South America. About 90 percent of the students are from families living below the poverty line. In 1988 the school's fifth graders were about two years behind grade level in reading and language arts and more than a year behind grade level in mathematics. By the spring of 1991 Hollibrook fifth graders were performing at grade level in all subjects and were one year above grade level in mathematics (McCarthy and Still, 1993).

Most of the accelerated schools have been established in the past two years, so it is too early for them to have completed their transformations. Nevertheless, the early results for these schools are also impressive. Investment in the education of at-risk students has a large payoff, and we have the wherewithal to use that investment wisely in accelerated schools. However, it does take a major commitment. What the Stanford project has demonstrated is that existing teachers, parents, and students in public schools can reorganize their schools and educational experiences so that virtually all children without major disabilities can become academically able. This can be done in a school that is joyful and exciting for all for the participants, with parents as active partners in the process. We must finally discard remediation and acknowledge its failure. In its place we must embrace treating all children as gifted and talented, and building on those strengths through acceleration.

Finally, it is paradoxical that many economists immediately resort to a market approach in looking for economic insights on improving the education of at-risk students (Friedman, 1962; Levin, 1991). Typically, they cite the work of Chubb and Moe (1990) or Coleman and Hoffer (1987), reanalyzed by Willms (1985), who found that students in Catholic schools were able to achieve a one-tenth of a standard deviation advantage over similar students in public schools. But accelerated schools have shown achievement gains of 1.5 standard deviations, or 15 times that large, without resorting to a change in educational finance to vouchers or other systems that would provide financial assistance to private schools. No public/private comparison has come close to finding this effect.

5

Keynoters and Award Recipients: An Open Exchange

With the terms of the debate established by Dr. Finn and Dr. Levin, Milken Family Foundation National Educator Award recipients gathered for an informal question-and-answer period with the keynote speakers. The session was moderated by Dr. Lewis C. Solmon, president of the Milken Institute for Job & Capital Formation.

Q: Dr. Finn, would you please comment on the role of early childhood programs?

Dr. Finn: One of the national goals established by President Bush is that every child should start school ready to learn, and I think that is in many ways the toughest and perhaps the most important goal to achieve because it may be the key to reaching the others. To achieve this goal a lot of children are going to need to learn more than they're currently learning *before* they get to school. That can sometimes be done through organized preschools; it can sometimes be done through well-run day-care programs; it can sometimes be done by well-run parents; and it can sometimes be done through other kinds of community and social services. But to achieve it, schools also need to be very clear about what *readiness* means. What does it mean to be ready for a given school? And how do you signal that to the parents of children who will one day be attending that school?

Q: Would you address the issue of choice and how it might prevent racial or ethnic violence?

Dr. Finn: Many of the questions surrounding the issue of choice are hard to figure out. Many of the best integrated schools in the country, both socially and economically, are schools of choice. They include magnet schools and other kinds of public choice schools and many private schools, such as the Catholic parochial schools, which in a great many urban areas do a superb job of racial and social integration. Some of the *least* integrated schools in America today are public school systems in places like Beverly Hills and Scarsdale, New York, which are superbly segregated by virtue of residence. In fact, what we have are little Berlin Walls all over the United States at the boundaries of school districts. Germany managed to tear down the Berlin Wall in Berlin, but we haven't torn most of ours down. So I don't think we should be too sanguine about the conflict. I think choice will serve to reduce barriers to racial and social integration for those people who face the worst barriers—poor people. Rich people already exercise choice. Poor people, generally speaking, cannot. I think that's a fundamental injustice and one we should be changing.

Q: What are your thoughts on contradictory reports that class size affects student achievement? As a former second-grade teacher, I know that if half of my children were out with chicken pox, I could have gotten twice as much done, especially with a classroom of 30 students.

Dr. Levin: There probably is some effect, but research shows only a modest effect. We need to transform the school to take advantage of different class size configurations. As a way of transforming American education, it's very, very expensive, and I think that most of the evidence would suggest that its impact is only moderate.

In California we have the largest class sizes in the country. Schools such as the Daniel Webster School have an average of 29 students per class at the elementary level. Now those classes are too large, and I'm not advocating classes that size, but I don't believe that class size is the main restriction to transforming schools. I would like to create a school that is full of excitement and support for all people, and a school that has direction, vision, and a spirit of working together.

Many of our schools have found solutions by generating that process. In California, for example, we have a lot of senior citizen communities whose residents are often looking for ways to be in contact with children. Many of them, by the way, are teachers and retired educators. When such people are brought into the classroom, class size is reduced in a very effective way. [At our schools] we also increase the numbers of teachers in training in our classes to help reduce class size, and we do a lot of work in groups. There are a lot of ways of dealing with the problem besides just mechanically reducing the class size by a few students and then expecting something dramatic to happen.

Q: My question deals with the privatization of public schooling, and Dr. Finn's Edison Project is a prime example. Dr. Finn's remarks were titled "Whither Education Reform?" and I wonder, if privatization becomes a reality, would we have something more like "*wither* education reform" without the *h*?

Dr. Finn: A lot of things that we do in education today are in some sense privatized, and I'm talking about things we do in public education as well. This Retreat is one example. But consider the list: the private use of security guards, the private bringing in of lunch services, the purchasing of books and materials from private vendors, the employing in many cases of private doctors or psychologists or others to provide part-time services in schools. You can go right on down the list of things that we do in public education that involve at least some degree of privatization or utilization of the private sector. I think, on the whole, those work well. In fact, I think in many cases they work better than their counterparts that are completely confined to the public sector.

It is also reasonable to ask what other aspects of education might work better if we had more vendors or suppliers or if we were providing them in different ways, including, incidentally, little professional service corporations of teachers who might get together and sell their services to a school or school system. There are a whole lot of ways we could break the mold of the traditional arrangement in which the public school system owns and employs everything it does. In fact, that mold's been cracked almost everywhere, and I think it's a good idea, rather than a bad idea, to see whether it could yield greater gains if we're willing to organize it in different ways.

Dr. Levin: Well, obviously I'm on the dubious side here. My suspicion is that the Edison Project is going to do some very creative things and much better things than the example I'm going to give you, but we already have a choice system between the public and private sector in terms of children's television. In the private sector it's called commercial TV, and in the public one it's called educational TV. I'd like people to compare the quality of *Sesame Street* with the typical menu of cartoons offered on Saturday morning; or compare *Nova* with MTV. Now, the fact of the matter is that the private sector is extremely sensitive to its audience, so if parents don't want a program for their children, all they have to do is turn the channel or turn the TV off. They don't even need to pay for transportation as you would if you were to choose among private schools. For some reason, however, they don't turn it off. For some reason this kind of commercial television is supported because it's exactly what provides the largest audiences. So when it comes to the 20 hours a week that Dr. Finn talks about that children watch television, all these parents out there who are trying to get the best schooling for their children somehow feel that it is fine for them. Frankly, commercial television has far more support and a far larger audience than the high-quality offerings on the public channels. And I don't think anyone at this Retreat would seriously state that the average or even the best 10 percent of commercial television is comparable with *Nova* or *Sesame Street*. So, I'm very, very dubious.

Q: Does a common core of knowledge and its common standards imply a national curriculum, nationwide testing, and school-by-school reporting of results? And, if so, what should that assessment look like?

Dr. Finn: Those things don't have to be national. Every one of those things could occur at the state level or even at the local level, and if they did I would be content. There are, in fact, some downsides to having them happen at the national level. I've been very impressed by the efforts made here in California, for example, with respect to curriculum frameworks for the children of this state and with respect to trying to make the state assessment program reflect honestly those frameworks while also getting beyond the bubble, so to speak, of the nature of the assessment instruments.

There is still a way to go, but, it seems to me, California has embarked in that direction, and I think usefully so. This has not, of course, happened in every state, and there's a good deal of talk about trying to work it out at the national level. The National Council on Education Standards and Testing, a bipartisan group of elected officials, educators, and others, recommended recently that there be national standards for content and for student performance and that these be set not by the federal government, but by essentially professional organizations, such as what the National Council of Teachers of Mathematics has done in math. That seems to be everybody's favorite example so far of what this might look like. The federal government has made grants to several organizations to try to do the same thing in science and in history. Obviously they'll be voluntary, and obviously if people don't think they make any sense, they won't use them. There's no coercion in using these standards.

Interestingly, the testing site is much more complicated. The council has come out with the idea that there ought to be a nationwide system of exams, not a single national test. A nationwide system, however, would produce a lot of different exams that would nevertheless be comparable to each other. The results could be reported nationally while allowing for local comparisons.

As to the nature of the assessment, we are very much in flux in this country right now. Almost everybody has recognized the limitations of the traditional multiple-choice test; and almost everybody has some good ideas about what other and better forms of assessment might look like; and almost everybody is also struggling with the difficulties that arise when you try to go beyond the bubble. I think we'll work our way through those difficulties eventually, but it's going to take a while.

Q: Dr. Levin, in many states special education programs are mandated. How do these special students fit into your accelerated schools program?

Dr. Levin: There is a problem when you generalize about special education, because you're generalizing about a very heterogeneous group of students and programs. The vast majority of special education children are in the so-called learning disabled group. There are others, of course, in other groupings, some with very specialized needs, such as being sight impaired or orthopedically handicapped.

We try to honor the appeal of Senate Bill 94-142 (the Education for All Handicapped Children Act of 1974) by making sure that all children are in the least restrictive environment possible. But we find that huge numbers of so-called learning disabled children are in fact misdiagnosed and misplaced. A child, for example, who hasn't been exposed to a lot of language or to certain spatial concepts and the like is often not likely to do very well on evaluations at an early age; so the real issue should be, Can the child learn these things, and can the child learn these things quickly? But an awful lot of children assigned to special education in fact have been misassigned; so in principle, we believe those children should be in regular classrooms but in a situation where you have so-called pull-in services.

Indeed, all of our special-needs people—Chapter 1 and migrant families and special education folks and bilingual folk—come in and work with the regular teachers on developing thematic curricula. Then, when they come in, at the time the children are divided into groups or doing individual research projects, all children are working with different adults, so there's no stigmatization. More important, the special-needs teachers are working on that thematic unit; that is, they do not have a set of vocabulary or readings that is simply outside of the overall thematic unit that the child is working in. That's what our schools try to do, as much as possible. We do have schools, though, that have special day classes in which they get involved in the overall instruction program of the school for only a portion of the day or in certain special activities.

Q: What should the role of state and federal governments be in school reform, funding, standards, mandates, and regulations?

Dr. Finn: That's another big one. The states, as you all know, have a constitutional responsibility to provide education. They've given it to themselves, and most of them are trying to carry it out. The federal government is a Johnny-come-lately to the education scene, and currently contributes 6 cents of the education dollar. The states currently account for about 50 cents of the public school dollar and localities for about 44 cents of the public school dollar. Those are national averages. Obviously, they vary a lot by state, but I think in very crude terms the relative amounts of influence and leverage are proportional to the percentages of financing that are supplied by each of these three levels of education. States have become by far the most active education reform initiators over the past few years—not all states, but many of them. There's been I think a good deal of useful stirring at the national level, but, in my view, that's about all the national level is capable of doing. I don't think it's capable of taking over. It doesn't award diplomas or buy textbooks or hire teachers. But without the time to go through an itemization of the various roles at issue, I don't think I'm going to be able to address this further.

Q: Dr. Finn, we see you as something of a theoretician. How would you put your theories into practice?

Dr. Finn: My friend Dennis Doyle occasionally describes think tanks as places where reality is examined to see if it conforms to theory. But, seriously, I think that's another giant question, each piece of which would take us a while to answer. I'm not trying to duck the question, I'm just trying to say that the realities of translating these theories into practice are going to be decided place by place; they're not going to be decided by a theoretician saying here's how you ought to implement them. I think one of the common themes Dr. Levin and I have sounded today is the degree to which these changes must be tailored to the individual circumstances and to the teams of people who are putting them into practice.

Q: Dr. Levin, to what degree do you feel that the theories you have presented will become widespread in the United States?

Dr. Levin: When you say "theories," I'd have to say that if in five years one's program has doubled each year to include 150 schools, and if one has clear results as we do, I think it goes beyond theory. My own view is that design *is* implementation. You can't talk about these drawing-board designs such as America 2000 and assess at the end of the year if we make improvements for two reasons: The end-of-the-year evaluation is so complex, and education is interactive. So we try to combine theory and practice all the time. We encourage collaboration and feedback. Sometimes we make mistakes, and then we try to correct them. We just keep working at it. This is a social movement and we *are* going to change the schools. That's it.

Q: In your paper, Dr. Finn, you indicated that every moral, well-educated adult is a potential teacher. We'd like you to elaborate on that and describe specifically what you think it takes to be a good teacher.

Dr. Finn: I think what it takes to be a good teacher is knowledge of subject, knowledge of and mastery of means of conveying that subject, love for children, and sound personal character. It also takes a degree of energy, enthusiasm, and hope. I think that combination of qualities is rare, I think it is not confined to the graduates of approved teacher education programs, and I think that it's reasonable to enlarge the pool of people who we at least consider as potential teachers.

The last time I looked there were about 27 million adults walking around this country with college degrees in their pockets. Some part of that population, in addition to the two and a half million people who are currently teaching, some of the other 24 million or so adults with college degrees, can plausibly be thought of as teachers. I think we should enlarge the pool and look for the best people we can find who have those qualities I briefly enunciated.

Q: Who should initiate the improvement programs for the 91 percent of children's nonschool time?

Dr. Finn: The difficulty with the 91 percent is that *nobody* is ultimately responsible for it. The most important source of leverage with respect to the individual child, however, is the parent. With respect to the community as a whole, we need a mechanism that we don't have in most communities to figure out a communitywide strategy for dealing with what children need. That communitywide strategy is going to have to become the property of a communitywide leadership cadre that I hope is going to represent a very substantial array of people and organizations.

Indeed, if we were organized to deal with the 91 percent right now we wouldn't have the problems we're having, so we're going to need to be organizationally inventive and create mechanisms that we don't typically have in place today. I think it would be terrific if educators and school systems were part of those mechanisms, and in fact, I don't think they can avoid being part of it, but I don't think they should be the only mechanism.

Q: Dr. Levin, what would you do with those teachers who do not perform up to par?

Dr. Levin: We've never had that problem because the problem handles itself. You see, as long as you have a lot of people who are very unhappy and dissatisfied, the malingerer, the one who's not doing his or her job, is simply tolerated. But when you start to work in groups to change the school, to participate, to work on problem solving, the malingerer or the one who doesn't have those competencies soon gets a little advice from colleagues about whether he or she wants to be in that kind of environment. In the spirit of what Dr. Finn has said, it seems to me that is fine. We shouldn't simply assume that anyone who is a teacher or on the staff in the school system should just be assigned to a given situation.

Now, at the same time, if a very few people are asked to be transferred, you have 10 times that number who want to get into the school because they hear about what is happening from their colleagues in the school. So it's a nonproblem.

Q: Dr. Finn, please define the term *punishment* as used in your paper.

Dr. Finn: I said there should be two kinds of consequences as part of any accountability system. There should be the warm, fuzzy kind that rewards success, and there should be the interventionist kind that, in the absence of success, seeks to make things change. I think that applies whether you have an individual child who is not learning something we hoped he or she would learn or a principal whose school is not up to snuff or a chief state school officer whose state is doing a really dreadful job. I think there should be interventionist consequences in which we seek to change an unsatisfactory situation, and the nature of the consequence is going to vary with the situation.

6

Teacher Leadership for Creating Innovative Schools

Linda Darling-Hammond

Teacher leadership is essential to the task of restructuring American schools for the twenty-first century. There is no other way to create the schools that we, as a nation, would like to have for educating all students for the increasingly complex and technological world we live in. Over the past 20 years, our society has tried to produce good schools by enacting ever more prescriptive legislation. One thing we have learned from those efforts is that regulations cannot transform schools. Only teachers can do that, in concert with parents, students, and administrators.

As Roland Barth (1990) has noted, many of the world's most fundamentally important leaders were teachers: Socrates, Plato, Moses, Jesus, and Ghandi, to name but a few. Barth envisions the school of tomorrow as a community of leaders, a place in which students, teachers, parents, and administrators all become school leaders in various ways. Leadership, in that sense, is the quality that enables people to make happen those things they believe in. If the wonderful things that occur in the classrooms of the Milken Family Foundation National Educator Award recipients are to reach students in all of their classrooms and in all of our schools, it will be because of the leadership these individuals exert in their schools and their communities, as well as in the profession of education.

Many educators are already engaged in serious initiatives to restructure education, as states and districts across the United States are seeking to invent schools for the twenty-first century. These schools have to meet new demands under new circumstances. I think that what is going on in today's educational reform movement is that we are in a struggle to invent a form of schooling for the twenty-first century that can replace the bureaucratic form of schooling that was created to meet the needs of the twentieth century. The organization that we created and have used to achieve our goals of 100 years ago has developed many complex ways to offer education to students.

But the goal of schooling has changed since the creation of twentieth-century schools. The mission of schools for the twenty-first century is not merely to "offer education," but to connect with all learners. And the new mission of teaching is not merely to "cover the curriculum," but to effect meaningful and productive and inventive forms of learning for all students. That is a new mission for schools, and one that can be enacted only with incredibly knowledgeable, competent, and empowered teachers who can teach students as well as subjects, who can create that magical bridge between learners' needs, talents, and experiences and challenging curriculum goals. This mission will rely on the capacity of teachers to create schools that focus primarily on the needs of learners and the demands of learning rather on regularized rules, procedures, and schedules.

And, of course, this mission must be tackled under new and more difficult social circumstances. The changes in our students, families, and society are well known. One of every four American students lives in poverty; half a million are homeless; an increasing number are members of traditionally underserved minority groups and newly arrived immigrants (Children's Defense Fund, 1991; National Coalition for the Homeless, 1987). June and Ward Cleaver are no longer the prototypical parents in the American household. "The Beav" does not go home to cookies and milk and someone to help him with his homework every night. That family model represents only 10 percent of American families today, and schools have to reinvent themselves in such a way that they create a family environment to support students in their learning.

Goals of School Restructuring

There are three major themes of school reform that will propel the school restructuring agenda for the next decade or so (see Newman, 1991). The first is the theme of creating *learner-centered schools,* which are more personalized, are focused on learners' needs rather than on standardized procedures, and are more flexible in how they approach different learning styles and approaches, less bureaucratized and fragmented. This means allowing teachers and others within the schools to take on the task of organizing themselves to work with students in ways that will be as effective as possible in addressing the whole child and in looking at learning holistically, rather than fitting students and teaching into fragmented structures that generally do not allow teachers to work with particular students for more than one year or, in high schools, for more than 40-minute segments in the day.

The second theme is teacher professionalism, the most important prerequisite of creating *knowledge-based schools*. These will be schools that are organized to build on what is known about teaching, learning, curriculum, and human development—schools that are developmentally appropriate and cognizant of both how children learn and how different teaching strategies can address their needs. These will be schools that are built with a strong, well-prepared, and carefully inducted profession of teachers at the foundation. They will be schools where teachers have the opportunity to work intensively with each other—planning, team teaching, making decisions about school design, collaborating on curriculum development, and ongoing assessment throughout the course of the day, the week, and the year.

Third is the theme of creating schools that can be genuinely accountable to and for students, that are *responsible and responsive* to the children, families, and communities they serve. These schools will employ forms of student and school assessment that are pointed at higher-order thinking and performance skills—rather than learning by rote and practice drills—along with more authentic means of achieving accountability than simply collecting statistics and reporting them. Genuinely accountable schools will be engaged in continual inquiry about practice and in ongoing teacher assessment of students regarding how they are growing, learning, and performing. They will open many-channeled communications among all of the members of the school community.

The effort to create learning- and learner-centered schools requires changing the nature of school reform efforts: Rather than trying to make our bureaucratic system work harder by enacting more mandates, as legislatures did throughout the 1970s and 1980s, the challenge is to focus on learners, mapping their needs to figure out what structures will allow them to engage in meaningful, well-supported learning. Among other things, this may mean rearranging schedules to allow more time for in-depth and cross-disciplinary learning, for more challenging forms of hands-on work, for greater opportunities for team teaching and team planning.

These new goals for schooling require a shift in our approach to school reform, from one that pursues top-down, standardized solutions to one that acknowledges the need for local energy, ideas, and flexibility; from efforts to improve schools by creating better regulations to initiatives that support and invest in better teaching. Over the course of the 1970s and 1980s, we learned that teacher-proofing as a strategy for improving education is fundamentally flawed. It is flawed because it assumes that children all learn in the same way, at the same rate, under the same circumstances, and that one can prescribe a package ahead of time that will work the same for all students. As all educators know, students are absolutely unique and definitely nonstandardized. As a consequence, standardized teaching or standardized practice is essentially malpractice, because the most effective teaching has to address itself to the individual learning needs, learning styles, ideas, cultures, experiences, and interests of the children with whom teachers work.

The kinds of changes that society wants and schools need cannot be mandated. They can be accomplished only by investing in teachers' knowledge and their capacity to make responsible judgments in the complex work of teaching and in the work of transforming schools.

That is one reason why, in the long run, improving schools is going to depend on transforming teaching into a full profession, just as occupations such as medicine, architecture, law, engineering, and others have done over the course of the century. We will not get knowledge-based and child-centered schools in which teachers can adapt their teaching to the needs of all children by enacting alternate forms of teacher certification that bring teachers into the occupation with only a few weeks of preparation and little knowledge of what students need and how they learn. We will not get more responsible schools by pretending that programs such as Teach for America, that bring in people with very little experience and knowledge, can solve the problems of American education.

We will get better schools by investing in enhanced teacher preparation programs and more meaningful licensing and certification processes; in selection practices that enable teachers to select their peers based on their expertise and commitment; in evaluation practices that enable teachers to engage in peer coaching and peer support; in mentoring programs that allow expert veterans to take responsibility for inducting new entrants into the profession and ensuring that those who receive tenure are those who should be in the teaching profession. When these professionalizing policies are enacted on a wide scale, and teachers begin to make decisions about how schools should operate so that they best serve the needs of students, we will then have the kinds of schools for the twenty-first century that can realize the goals of the restructuring movement.

The National Center on Organization and Restructuring of Schools at the University of Wisconsin lists six of these major goals. One is *authentic student achievement,* meaning the kinds of student work that engage students themselves in investigation, design, construction, inquiry, invention, and the production of new solutions. These kinds of achievements can be evaluated through portfolios of student work, extended projects, and complex performance tasks rather than multiple-choice tests or other forms of evaluation that involve student retrieval of discrete pieces of information.

A second goal is *equity*. Achieving this goal will require creating schools in which all students—students of diverse backgrounds, interests, cultural experiences, and family situations—have equal opportunity to learn because the school respects their experiences and potentials and teaches to their multiple intelligences and multiple strengths. These schools will provide a rich and challenging curriculum that is taught in ways that acknowledge the multiple approaches to learning and ways of knowing that characterize diverse learners and relies upon multiple modes of performance and assessment.

A third goal is *empowerment*. As you well know, research on organizational productivity in many contexts, including business, industry, and government, has indicated the need to decentralize decision making. The assumption that the best decisions are made by the people who have to implement and live with them has proved true in businesses that have restructured. The empowerment of teachers and other members of local school communities in school-based management initiatives draws on what has been learned about the effectiveness of quality work circles, total quality management techniques, and other strategies that invest the power to identify, frame, and solve problems in the people who are closest to the work.

The fourth goal is the creation of the *communities of learning*. There is a felt need throughout this society and in governments around the world to transform impersonal, fragmented, bureaucratic organizations into organizations in which participants share goals and pursue a common agenda of activities through collaborative work involving stable, personalized contact over the long term. In communities of learning, all students and teachers feel included as participants in the school. Teachers and students relate to one another in less specialized roles and more as whole persons. They participate and take responsibility for the collective life of the school and can count upon one another for help in meeting both individual and group needs.

When I was a high school English teacher, I learned how difficult it was to build communities of learning in traditional secondary school organizations. I struggled with the realities of the school structure that we currently have. Like my colleagues, because I taught 150 students daily, marching through my classroom in groups of 30 at a time, I found I could not be responsible to each of those students in the way I wished to be. I could be responsible for teaching tenth-grade English—that is, covering the subject—but not for reaching every student in a personal and individual way. Even as I saw the needs many of those students brought, I could not address them effectively without changes in the structure. I yearned for an option that would allow me to work with the same group of students for two or three years. In this way, I could come to know students, their needs, and their families well. I could also work with smaller groups of students in an interdisciplinary fashion for longer periods of the day. Without those kinds of structured changes, I knew I could never be fully responsive to the needs of students as individuals.

The restructuring that is going on in many American schools today will transform the ways we put adults and children together in schools to create communities of learning. We will increasingly invent schools in which teachers can work with students over longer periods of time, to create relationships and connections that can overcome the alienation that otherwise can exist in schools and overwhelm both teachers and students.

The fifth goal is to invent ways to engage in *reflective dialogue*. One of the things we are beginning to learn about student and adult learning, about teaching and social change, is that belief systems cannot be changed by unilateral imposition or replacement of an old belief with a new belief. Most teachers have probably been in as many staff development meetings as I have in which someone announces, "Today we are going to do X"—whatever the newest fad is—and one is then expected to behave in ways that are different from all of the practices one engaged in before. Research has now demonstrated what many of us already knew—that that approach is completely ineffective in transforming peoples' beliefs or behaviors. Instead, beliefs change through dialogue that stimulates open and nonthreatening questions, and through opportunities to test assumptions by exposure to new experiences. The failure of many curriculum reforms can be explained by their neglect of this point. Typically, curriculum packages have been developed in isolation from teachers, who were then expected simply to implement them. In short, mandates, regulations, and materials are not enough. We will transform schools as we create opportunities to enrich dialogues within them.

The final area for change is *accountability*. The accountability theme, as it is now being discussed in many states and localities, represents a shift in thinking about how to enhance educational quality. There is currently a widely discussed idea that we ought to switch from regulating the process of education to an approach that sets clearer goals for outcomes and then invents more effective ways to achieve those outcomes. As this theme and ways of implementing it are debated and tried in the years to come, it will be incredibly important for teachers to engage in these accountability debates and arguments, to define and redefine what "genuine accountability for student learning" means.

Teachers must articulate what conditions are necessary to create schools where no student can fall through the cracks and what the requirements are for creating and sustaining personalized and learner-centered schools. Teachers must be at the forefront of discussions about what it means to value and evaluate authentic student achievement, achievement that represents meaningful and active learning on the part of the students. Educators must be involved in setting that agenda or that agenda will be poorly set. It will devolve into mechanistic approaches that rely on batches of numbers and statistics, an array of measurements of things that ultimately fail to get to the heart of what it means to help a child learn or to create a good school.

The Tasks of Teacher Leaders

Changes in practice, changes in policy, and changes in the profession are the three areas in which teachers and other educators can help us find our way to the twenty-first century. Many are already working on these changes. A vision of changes in all three of these areas produced by a group of teachers in an organization called Impact II (1991) displays one view of the future:

> It is now sometime in the future—more than 20 but less than 100 years from now. The "schools" we see are no longer the isolated schools of the 1990s but rather campus-style community learning centers . . . with sport centers, playing fields, a public library, and medical and social support systems services. . . . There are well-equipped laboratories for inquiry-based research, language labs, planning rooms, performance areas, animal habitats, . . . greenhouses that provide produce for the food plaza. (p. 8)
>
> All classrooms are arranged for collaborative cooperative school work. . . . Adults explore new career options while they help to teach the young. Older people share their wisdom as they continue to learn. Groups of all ages discuss ideas, problems and community issues. The goal is to learn to be "lifelong" learners and teachers in a community that honors education. (pp. 8-9)
>
> With the help of . . . community mentors, students carry on significant investigative work, making decisions to solve problems and answer meaningful questions that impact on themselves, their peers and their communities. . . . Students integrate learning experiences that cut across formerly discrete and often isolated disciplines in a learning center that is truly interdisciplinary. (p. 9)

> Teachers design and implement large-group instruction. They also spend a considerable part of any day advising students' learning projects, conferencing with individual students and small groups, and collaborating with other professionals in support of students completion of a meaningful learning goal, mutually agreed upon. (p. 8)

This type of structure for teachers' work is beginning to exist in American schools as it has for many years in other parts of the world, such as Asia and Europe. In most such schools, teachers are engaged in working with large groups of students only about one-third of the workweek (15 out of 40-45 hours). The rest of the time they work with other teachers on curriculum planning and on developing assessments for students, and meet with parents, individual students, and small groups. This kind of work organization does not necessarily cost more, but it does require rethinking the way we use professional staff in schools. It requires moving away from a system in which one out of every two education dollars is spent outside of the classroom on a variety of specialists and offices that inspect and report and monitor teaching work rather than on performing teaching work. It requires bringing those resources that currently sit in offices outside the classroom into the classroom, so that teaching work can be structured around the learning of teachers and students together.

> Assessment of student work is carried out by the community of learners based on the student's mastery of specific skills necessary to taking one's place in the world. Both student and teacher evaluate the work the student has generated. The peer group plays a key role as well in offering feedback to other students whose work they have shared and critiqued in its various stages. (p. 13)
>
> Businesses are tightly woven into the fabric of learning. They offer classes in financial and career planning, accept student interns, . . . endow classroom labs, volunteer teachers, pay for "chairs" for educators, allow time for parent-employees to work with their children in school and conference with teachers, and provide day care for the children in their community. (p. 15)

Professional teachers will have a comprehensive education for their multiple roles, including

> knowledge of child development, learning theory, teaching modalities and curriculum development . . . Teachers will also take on new areas of study focusing on family and community, leadership theory, problem solving and conflict resolution, and teacher evaluation. (p. 9)

> Education schools are no longer at colleges but located within the public school setting. This new alignment allows for collaboration and learning among new teachers, experienced educators and school-based, research-oriented professors. (p. 11)
>
> At the school level, all decisions regarding staffing are made by teachers, who will also hire personnel to carry out administrative functions. The primary challenge in our future will be to design positions that directly support and impact on the learning process. (p. 15)
>
> Teachers must develop new ways of assessing their own performance, (e.g., peer evaluation) as well as that of their students, so the public will know that its investment is paying off. (p. 18)

Every one of these features of the vision of the future currently exists in at least some schools that are being revitalized and restructured today. The Milken Family Foundation National Educator Award recipients are all involved in various ways in making this vision a reality.

Of course, this work is not easy. The concept of teacher leadership violates old norms and conventions among administrators and, frequently, teachers as well. Moving from the isolation of the classroom to public discussion and activity focused on changing student learning opportunities is a big step that does not happen naturally. It requires a great deal of individual and organizational change—and change does not happen without learning.

Quite often what appears to be resistance to change is really a function of a lack of experience and understanding. If we think about how students learn, we can see that they change based on how teachers expand their experience and their view of what is possible. In the same way, educators can start initiatives for promoting learning within our schools by collecting data and envisioning new possibilities. We can start by asking, How do students experience this school? What is possible? How can we build new practices? If we want our colleagues in our schools and in our profession to think with us, we also have to help them expand their own experiences, and thus expand the possibilities for schools in which they can engage with us in a continual study of learning. We have to begin to envision schools not as the *targets* of change, as much policy making has done in the past, but rather as *centers* of change.

Examples of Teacher Leadership

I would like to give some examples of how some teachers have been involved in changing practices in their own schools, in their districts, and in the profession. The first kind of understanding that is central in doing this kind of work is how important it is to expand teachers' imaginations, interests, and experiences. All of us start with what we know. One of the lessons of our field's growing understanding of learning is that it is constructed from the experiences and mental frameworks that we already have. This is true whether we are talking about children or adults. Thus, change follows from expanding experience and what is known.

Dawn Harris-Martine is a teacher in Harlem, New York. Her work in bringing whole-language instruction into her classroom has brought about outstanding results with students who in other classrooms often failed to learn to read and to write effectively. Harris-Martine's achievements have been so remarkable that her work has been featured in books and videotapes used for research and staff development. Her second-grade students are reading novels and writing full and highly developed collections of stories, poems, and other works of literature. Though engrossed in her own work, Harris-Martine began to think about the other classrooms in her school. She began to wonder how she could work with other teachers in a way that would allow their students to experience these kinds of learning opportunities.

Harris-Martine experienced a lot of resistance—feelings that "maybe you can do that, but that kind of teaching does not apply to me"—in the school. Nonetheless, with a few interested colleagues, she started a noontime reading group in which adult literature was read. By dis-cussing the books they had selected, by using reading logs to explore their own literature-based experience, the group eventually found itself engaged in discussions of reading in the classroom. Soon discussions centered on how to allow children the same kind of joy and engagement in literature the teachers themselves were experiencing. Within two years, changes in the classrooms brought about by this experience were remarkable throughout Harris-Martine's school. Every classroom was engaged, worksheets were decreasing in number, and opportunities for children to engage good literature, to discuss, to write, and to make those experiences their own had increased. Eventually, schoolwide change has en-abled that school to go from being one of the lowest-achieving schools in its district to one of the highest.

There is a principle of change that we keep rediscovering: If you can extend and expand teachers' own experience and capacity for a certain kind of learning, then you expand their possibilities for engaging that kind of practice with children. The Bay Area Writing Project is one example of a program that follows from a similar kind of understanding of how people change, practice, and learn. Teachers engaged in their own writing and in the journey created by the writing process are enabled to help children learn to write in more meaningful and authentic ways.

Another example of this principle is in evidence in a school called the International High School in New York City. The school serves only those students whose first language is not English and who initially score below the twentieth percentile on an English language test. The remarkable success experienced with these students is partly a result of the student assessment techniques used, which rely heavily on extended projects, portfolio work, hands-on cooperative learning experiences, self-assessment, and peer evaluation among the students. These practices became possible in the school because the faculty, in developing its own teacher evaluation system, decided to use portfolios, self-assessment, and peer coaching as the bases for their own teacher evaluation process. By engaging in that kind of work themselves, they began to find the possibilities for extending the same experience to students. Other changes in practice—for example, with cooperative learning opportunities for students—also tended to derive from the opportunity of teachers to engage in collaborative and cooperative work at the school level. It is unusual to see practices in classrooms that teachers have not experienced as adults in their own work and learning environments.

Shared decision making and school reform represents another avenue for teacher involvement in the process of change. Across the country, schools are being asked to engage in site-based management and shared decision making, along with a variety of approaches to school self-assessment and needs assessment. The key to exercising leadership in these areas is to start with questions rather than solutions, to stimulate inquiry rather than seek predetermined answers. One might start, for example, with questions such as, How do we accommodate differences in student learning now? Why do we use the instructional practices that we do? What suggests that our current practices are or are not effective, and in what ways? What other instructional practices are possible? And, to the extent that certain ideas present themselves, What then can we learn and know about those practices, and to what extent are they adaptable?

One of the things we have learned in looking at change processes is that knowledge is very personal. What each person knows is determined by what that individual has had experience doing. So the task of stimulating and supporting change is one of continually allowing people to start from where they are and to expand into new ways of thinking and doing.

I am reminded of the lessons learned in the 1930s, when the Progressive Education Association created a group of experimental schools, including 30 high schools, from which 300 colleges and universities agreed to accept students, based not on their grade point averages or "Carnegie units," but on students' own products and teacher recommendations. Among the participating universities were all of the land-grant universities in the country, as well as Ivy League universities such as Harvard, Princeton, and Yale. At the end of eight years, after the researchers had followed nearly 3,000 students into these colleges, they found, using a wide array of assessment measures, that students from the experimental schools outperformed students from traditional schools in almost all respects, ranging from academic performance to social responsibility, and from health and fitness to the ability to exercise leadership.

When they reexamined the experimental schools to figure out what made the difference, they found that there was no particular solution or fad or idea that differentiated the most successful from the least. Rather, it was the extent to which members of the school community had themselves engaged in the process of developing their own goals and committed themselves to thinking about how to shape the learning environment to achieve those goals. In fact, schools that had adopted ideas from consultants or other schools were less likely to produce major changes in student achievement, regardless of what the ideas were. (For more on these schools, see Aikin, 1942; Chamberlain, 1942.)

It is the process of engaging in reflection and inquiry that proves to be the most important element in transforming schools, and this is one of the areas in which the leadership of teachers in their schools will be especially needed and helpful. "Backward planning" is one of the ways in which many schools are trying to stimulate that process of reflection. This approach sets in motion planning processes in which school teams, program teams, or grade-level teams get together to start to discuss what they would like to see students doing and able to do. For example, they might decide: We would like students to write coherently and persuasively; to ask smart questions; to get information; to solve practical problems using mathematics; to use mathematics or other languages to express concepts and ideas; to read books for enjoyment and to stimulate their curiosity; to become good citizens; and so on.

The next step is figuring out what kinds of activities and concrete performance tasks would both develop and assess these abilities: writing persuasive essays, developing and implementing research plans, conducting a science experiment, conducting a survey and graphing the results, creating a small book, measuring the school yard, following a recipe, and on and on. Faculty plan these assessment tasks, which may become components of the students' portfolios or of exhibitions that are conducted in a public manner. When these tasks become a publicly available exemplar of what students are able to do, they represent goals that students and teachers can aim for together, and teaching becomes organized around the coaching needed to help students perform well. This kind of backward planning seems to create the atmosphere for inquiry and reflection—for looking at what we are doing and how we are doing it and what students are able to do as a result—that stimulates widespread school changes.

In addition to school change strategies, teachers are increasingly involved in creating schools. The Key School in Indianapolis was created by a group of teachers who decided to put to work the multiple intelligence theories of Howard Gardner (1983). In that school, teachers create activities each day that engage each of the seven intelligences of every child. In this way, teachers have an opportunity to find avenues of strength for every student, and to develop the full range of intelligences human beings possess and use.

Central Park East School in New York has grown from its beginnings in 1974—with a few teachers seeking to implement open education ideas in East Harlem—to four schools: three elementary schools and one high school all located in the East Harlem area. All of these schools were begun by teachers; each of them started small, with a group of like-minded educators, whose purpose was to ensure that students have the opportunity to experience a learner-centered and democratic form of education. Deborah Meier (1987), the teacher who began the first Central Park East School, has written this about that effort:

> One of our primary reasons for starting the school—although we didn't often say it—was our personal desire for greater autonomy as teachers. We spoke a lot about democracy, but we were also just plain sick and tired of having to negotiate with others, worry about rules and regulations, and so on. We all came together with our own visions—some collective and some individual—of what teaching could be like if only we had control. Ours was to be a teacher-run school. We believed that parents should have a voice in their children's schooling, and we thought that "choice" itself was a form of power. We also believed that we could be professionally responsive to parents and that, since the school would be open to parents at all times and the staff would be receptive, there would be plenty of opportunity to demonstrate our responsiveness. (p. 755)

There certainly was a lot of both progress and struggle before the schools reached where they are today. And now, the secondary school that grew out of that first elementary school has graduated a group of African-American and Latino students this year in a district that previously would have lost 50 percent of these students before graduation. Not only are they graduating but 92 percent are going on to four-year colleges and universities, and the rest are all going on to some form of postsecondary education (Walter, 1991). When teachers act on their beliefs, schooling can become a very different experience.

Previously at this Retreat, you heard about how these ideas could be carried into the policy arena. District and state policies need to be shaped—

and sometimes challenged—by teachers who understand what students need. This is beginning to happen in states across the country, in places like Vermont, where teachers have developed a portfolio system for evaluating students' work and have created local professional standards boards for evaluating their own profession, to states like California, Washington, Oregon, and many others. One of the happiest things about the recognition represented by the Milken Family Foundation National Educator Awards is that state superintendents will know who to call when they create commissions to rethink curriculum and assessment, when they look for ways to strengthen teacher licensing standards, when they consider how teacher education should be conducted.

It is important for teacher leaders to speak out, to take stands, and to write. It is increasingly true that teachers are writing and publishing in professional journals about how, why, and in what ways their work has proceeded. It is important for a number of reasons: to inform the field and strengthen our knowledge base, but also to transform research. The frame that researchers use for understanding practice and for making recommendations has to be informed and educated by the understanding and knowledge of teachers. One of the big tasks we must undertake as a collective profession is not just to put research into practice, but also to put practice into research.

Finally, it is important to participate in improving the profession. Teachers need to be involved in professional standards boards, in creating professional development schools for preparing and inducting new teachers, in participating in mentoring programs that help define what the teaching of the future will be like by preparing the teachers of the future, and in transforming selection and evaluation practices for teachers.

Real progress in these areas is finally under way. The new National Board for Professional Teaching Standards is going to begin to offer assessments one and a half years from now for the advanced certification of teachers at high levels of competence. This is the first national standards board for teaching that provides a voice like those that other professions have had for many decades. It consists of professional members, more than half of whom are classroom teachers and most of the remainder of whom are educators who have been classroom teachers. The board's assessments—using portfolios, performance tasks, and expert peers—will be the basis for building greater recognition and voice in the teaching profession as well.

The Future of Teaching and Public Education

Teaching now is at a crossroads. There are two futures at hand. One of these futures maintains the current features of teaching in the face of the major demographic and economic changes ahead of us and the expanding expectations of schools. In the year 2000 it looks something like this:

> After a brief flurry of education activities in the mid-1980s, schools settled back to business as usual. The education governors had come and gone. Educational leaders were relieved to have the commission reports out of the way. A period of teacher shortages had been addressed by increased use of emergency and alternate certification. By 1998, teachers' salaries had returned to the levels they had reached in the early 1970s (following the previous teacher shortage), but they declined once again thereafter. Teacher recruitment remained problematic; 46 states initiated quick alternate routes into teaching, and classrooms, especially in the cities, were staffed in that way.
>
> Throughout the 1990s students in public education changed, but schools did not. Great waves of immigration boosted the number of minorities and non-English-speaking children to nearly 40 percent of public school enrollment, and they were increasingly concentrated in poorly funded city school districts. Because the majority of the teaching staff in these districts had retired, and the large numbers of vacancies were hard to fill, shortages led to larger classes and more emergency hiring. The many teachers whose formal pedagogical preparation consisted of a six-week summer course desperately wanted to address the learning needs of their students, but their knowledge of child development, language acquisition, learning styles, and alternative teaching methods was too skimpy to provide them with adequate ammunition for the job.
>
> The public's periodic concern over low student performance was assuaged by the enactment of stiffer requirements: more frequently administered tests for students to determine promotion, placement, and graduation (because teachers could not be trusted to make those decisions); more highly specified grade-level objectives and curriculum activities matched to the standardized tests; tighter control on textbook adoptions; more rigid procedures for tightening school management; more record-keeping requirements for keeping tabs on administration, instruction, and student progress; and more frequent evaluation and testing of teachers.
>
> Teaching in public schools was increasingly determined by these regulatory requirements rather than by knowledge about teaching and the needs of learners. Teachers taught for the required multiple-choice tests from mandated texts and curriculum packages aligned with the tests. Students no longer read books, wrote papers, conducted experiments, or completed projects in class. Their learning was structured instead by worksheets, practice tests, packaged instructional modules, and more practice tests. Scores on basic skills tests continued to remain stable, but scores on tests of higher-order thinking continued to decline. More students were held

back and many dropped out. U.S. students continued to perform poorly relative to students in other countries on international assessments.

Earlier enthusiasm for reforms gave way to disillusionment and to lower school budgets as middle-class parents fled to private schools and the general population, consisting largely of older citizens without children in schools, voted down tax levies for education. Just as the progressive education initiatives in the 1960s had been replaced in the 1970s by the movement to cap taxes on school support and go back to the basics, so the restructuring rhetoric of the 1980s gave way to technocratic solutions less threatening to established bureaucracies. By the year 2000, public frustration with the schools resurfaced, with cries from the business community for employees who could function in an information-based economy. New commissions were born to declare the nation at risk once again.

Another vision, one that includes leadership from the teaching profession, is possible. In this future, teaching continues its progress toward becoming a profession that is student oriented and knowledge based. In the year 2000, a different public education system has emerged that looks something like this:

Much has changed since the last crisis in education in the 1980s. A second wave of reform impelled a new coalition among teachers, school administrators, and teacher educators, all of whom began thinking of themselves as members of the same profession with common goals. They articulated the first professional definition of teaching knowledge through the National Board for Professional Teaching Standards. This stimulated the creation of analogous state boards, which built upon the new vision to establish meaningful standards for teacher licensure and preparation in the states. Most states established professional internships for the clinical training of new teachers following the completion of a master's degree in teaching. Mentor teachers worked with these new teachers to make sure they would learn not just to cope, but to teach effectively. A number of states and districts created professional development schools, where all teachers in training were coached by these expert mentor teachers. The new cohort of teachers—more than a million strong—was better prepared than any that had preceded it.

Teacher shortages were met with higher salaries and differentiated staffing arrangements. These responses began to change the shape of school organizations and the allocation of school resources. As salaries climbed another 30 percent, to a level comparable with other professions for college-educated workers, the supply of prospective teachers willing and able to undergo rigorous preparation programs grew. As the qualifications of teachers increased, the perceived need to spend large amounts of education budgets on massive control and inspection systems diminished. Hierarchies that had developed to design, regulate, and monitor teaching flattened out. Teachers assumed more professional responsibilities, and schools took on new shapes conducive to professional teaching.

As in other professions, differentiated roles and responsibilities gradually emerged as a means of balancing the requirements of supply and qualifications. Those less extensively trained were able to perform the limited tasks for which they were prepared, but only in team-teaching situations under the supervision of career professionals who had full preparation. Such structures also promoted the kinds of consultation and peer review of practice that are essential to a professional role.

Members of the education profession insisted on selecting and inducting their own peers and on collectively deciding the best use of knowledge and resources to meet student needs. As serious induction and sustained professional development and collaboration in problem solving replaced the sink-or-swim, closed-door ethos of an earlier era, professional knowledge and effectiveness grew.

Instructional practices changed, too. The assembly-line approach to processing students gave way to more varied and appropriate ways of teaching and learning. Lectures and worksheets were no longer the preponderant school activities. Cooperative and experiential learning, projects, debates, essays, and exhibitions engaged students of various learning styles, encouraged students to construct and solve intellectual problems, and created more meaningful and useful ways of assessing students' progress. A wide variety of more productive approaches to organizing the school day and year and of grouping students gave individual teachers and students time together, reducing the pull-outs, pass-throughs, start-ups, and wind-downs that had stolen teaching time and had decreased teachers' capacities to come to know students well.

Incentives to attract the most expert teachers to the profession's greatest needs and challenges also emerged. Following the lead of path-breaking districts such as Dade County, Rochester, Louisville, and others, master teachers redesigned inner-city schools as exemplars of professional practice, where they coached new teachers, put research into practice and practice into research, and put state-of-the-art knowledge to work for kids. Equity and excellence became joined with professionalism.

By the year 2000, American education had begun to be transformed. The best American students performed as well as any in the world. The vast majority graduated with not only minimal basic skills, but also the capacity to write, reason, think analytically, invent, and create. Complaints from the business community about the quality of graduates subsided for the first time since World War II. And for the first time since the beginning of

> the twentieth century, a decade was launched without a chorus of commissions crying "crisis" in the American public schools. The road taken, as it turned out, was the one that finally made the difference.

The educators represented at this Retreat, and their colleagues, are the navigators of that road and the people who will make that difference. These are the folks who are going to create a world in which we will be able to say, for all teachers: "Those who can, do; those who understand, teach." And furthermore, "Those who can, teach; and those who can't, go into a less significant line of work."

7

Creating Innovative Schools: An Open Exchange

Having ignited keen interest in the concrete possibilities for creating innovative schools, Dr. Darling-Hammond answered questions from the floor.

Q: I wonder if you could comment on the position of textbook manufacturers and the suppliers of all the worksheets and textbooks we're going to be weaning ourselves from. Who is going to educate these people and bring *them* along? Do you imagine their lobbying against this type of movement? I imagine they're not going to give up a multimillion-dollar industry just because teachers want to change what we're doing.

Dr. Darling-Hammond: That's a loaded question. One way to answer it is to consider how to bring textbook publishers along. Another is to consider how, in the event that texts don't support the kind of learning you want to achieve, you deal with materials in other ways. Some teachers, confronted with texts they felt were not supportive of the kind of learning they were trying to achieve, set out to develop their own materials and texts in lieu of using what was available from textbook publishers. This happened recently in some parts of New York and also in California.

Another strategy is to educate textbook publishers while at the same time educating policy makers in your state—if you're an adoption state—as to what kinds of approaches are important and necessary. Textbook publishers, after all, try to meet the demands of the state agencies that adopt textbooks. The real leverage, then, comes with getting involved with that adoption process, with the state agency, and with being a part of specifying what ought to be in the text. If you're in California or Texas, you're in a powerful position because publishers pay attention to those states. If you're in Vermont, on the other hand, you're probably not going to leverage as many textbook publishers. You can also work with colleagues anywhere that specifications are being set.

Recently in California the teachers on the Textbook Adoption Committee for one of the new curriculum frameworks rejected *all* the texts brought to them in math, saying none of them did the trick. We won't have them, they said. And the publishers had to go back and start over. So it can be done.

Q: What is your prescription for sustaining and supporting agents of change in our schools when most of us are still in the I, me, and my mode instead of being in the we, us, and our mode necessary to invent solutions for today's world?

Dr. Darling-Hammond: Creating schools that are change makers can be very lonely work, and many of you have experienced that. An important aspect of doing that work is to be a part of a network of other teachers and folks in schools who are trying to go in similar directions. Both the AFT and the NEA have created networks for school reform that are ways of reaching out to teachers. The Center on Restructuring that I am involved in has also begun such a network, and in fact, they're available in different forms across the states. But these networks can also be created by teachers themselves.

In many places I know of, teachers have reached both within their schools and across to other schools in their neighborhoods and districts to invent their own networks to support each other as they effect change. They engage in study groups and in various kinds of professional development opportunities and speak out to the district about needed changes and district policy. By connecting even a dozen teachers across schools in a district, a very powerful voice can be had.

Q: Would you expand on your statement, "The public does not trust the standards it has set for teachers?"

Dr. Darling-Hammond: Among the several crises in education is teacher certification. It's my perception that, across the country, neither members of the profession, practicing teachers, nor members of the public—including legislators—believe that certification standards really separate those who can teach effectively and responsibly from those who cannot. I think it's because those standards are not credible that we have all of these attempts to create loopholes and differences in the standards.

Any of you who has ever had to change states in your teaching career may have encountered the unfortunate situation in which even veterans with 10 or 15 years of outstanding experience are forced to worry about taking one course or another as a means of getting engaged to teach. Because of this arrangement, we lose a lot of people from the profession entirely.

We frequently hear teachers say they have to do something or other to get certified, but one doesn't get the feeling that the certification process has separated what they *really* need to know from what they have to know to obtain the credential. Ultimately, if teaching is going to be a solid profession, it needs meaningful credentials established by the members of the profession—credentials that we really believe in and that are the basis for responsible practice.

To reach this point, several things must happen. One, teachers must be in a position to set standards. In all other professions but teaching, standards for licensure are set by professional standards boards populated by blue-ribbon members of the profession. This is true for lawyers, architects, accountants, doctors, nurses, and so on.

With respect to teaching, in most states those standards boards have not existed. In the past few years a dozen or so states *have* acquired them, and they need to begin to figure out how to act. The other states have done standard setting through their state departments of education. They've also set standards by means of course counting. It works sort of like a menu, and no other profession does that. No other profession specifies what courses you have to take.

Other professions set an outcome standard—the bar exam, the board certification exams for medicine, the architectural registration exam—that must be met for an individual to be licensed or certified. Many states *are* now beginning to think about moving in that direction.

The third important difference is that those exams are created by members of the profession, and they are typically very much performance based. Lawyers have to write an essay or a brief outlining how to resolve a case. Architects do design work; they design buildings on their exam. Psychiatrists are observed interviewing a patient, after which a jury of their peers decides if they've asked the right questions and come up with a reasonable diagnosis. Teachers, on the other hand, take a multiple-choice exam set by people outside of the profession. It is an approach that many states are beginning to tackle and change, and it is an approach the National Board is intending to create an alternative method for—set by teachers who will watch teachers teaching and reported on in ways that give us an authentic measure of their teaching skills.

Q: You have created a wonderful world of excitement for teachers. I'm a policy maker, a state senator from the state of Alaska. We're involved—particularly in my home community of Anchorage—in a major effort that joins businesses, schools, and educators in the process of reform. It's exciting, but it's still a question of money for the teachers and money for the schools. Do you have some comments on how we can affect the boards of education and the commissioners? The people who sit in the finance room and struggle with resources?

Dr. Darling-Hammond: You've asked two questions. First, what can policy makers do to support teachers in making change, and second, what do we do with the finances? They are great questions.

I think there are a number of strategies that state policy makers can use to support teachers in their efforts to make schools all that they can be. One is to look not only at the kind of strategies that will empower and stimulate schools to reflect on their practices and think differently, but also to evaluate previous policies that may need changing in order for new policies to have a chance. There is a tremendous policy collision in most states in which new ideas are layered on old ones. In order to make progress, we really have to rethink the structures of the past. Alaska actually does a lot of this. It's one of my favorite states in terms of policy for teachers.

Focusing on ways to engage members of the profession in the process of defining the profession is another piece of a favorable policy picture. Creating a professional standards board, challenging it to rethink preparation, licensure, professional development, and establishment of professional development schools and certification standards is clearly a role that state policy makers can take on. Thinking of practices in terms of their effectiveness for student learning is another strategy, whether through legislation or through school review processes in which participatory decision making will occur in schools. New York is among the states looking at adopting something like Great Britain's inspectorate system, whose external review process has friendly critics come into schools to look at practices, including those for engaging teachers in rethinking, reflecting, and reshaping. That kind of examination process helps schools think and learn about other strategies for their own change processes.

To respond to the second question and a major issue that everyone is facing: How do we deal with limited resources? There is a general need in American schools for key strategic changes in resource allocation. One has to do with the fact that we spend half of our resources outside the classroom in various parts of a hierarchy that is created to inspect, monitor, and report on teaching, but not to do teaching. Most countries spend 80 or 90 percent of their dollars in the classroom. These countries invest in greater teacher competence. They reduce the inspecting and reporting requirements outside of school by creating an expectation that teachers will know how to make responsible decisions. And, they operate with the understanding that teachers don't need to be monitored in order to do so. We must start getting a lot of that money outside of the superstructure and into the school.

Second, we must think about what parts of the system we may want to change and how we can invest in the future instead of in the past. One example of this exists in a local district in New York. (Where, by the way, our motto is, "If it moves, test it.") In this district there were some batteries of state-required standardized tests and 21 batteries of locally mandated standardized tests for children to get through between grades K and 12. We figured the district could have solved its budget crisis, which ultimately resulted in layoff of teachers, if they had cut the testing program in half. This reduction would not have resulted in the loss of any important information about students. So in facing the need for more authentic assessment in the future, we need to ask, Should we continue to make the trade-off of investing in assessments of the past? The question could apply to a lot of other practices. If we're aiming for more integrated education for children, should we continue to pour money into special education programs rather than try to create integrated, comprehensive services? How do we rethink the slots and the lines of budgets so that we're focusing on getting the services to children in the classroom?

Q: How teachers participate in review and evaluation processes is reminiscent of the guild system. How does your Center for Restructuring relate to teacher preparation at colleges and universities in New York, and how do they in turn relate to the state legislature?

Dr. Darling-Hammond: We are helping to support a network of several hundred professional development schools across the country. These represent efforts by universities to work directly with schools in creating sites for the preparation and student teaching internships of new teachers. We're also working with a number of organizations, such as the Holmes group, that are rethinking teacher preparations.

An important aspect of this effort, as you suggest, has to do with policy, because teacher education can't change much until licensure standards and state approval standards change. Our center is working with the Council for Chief State School Officers and with 40 states on a project concerning licensure standards for teachers. The aim is this: standards to accommodate a form of teacher education that supports teachers' knowledge about learners and learning and that creates opportunities for teachers to practice both under the guidance of expert, veteran teachers and in internship programs.

Q: Much educational reform and restructuring seems to be coming from institutions outside the profession and beyond policy makers. If this is the case, how can we as public educators recapture the initiative regarding what happens to us and what happens to children?

Dr. Darling-Hammond: That's a great question. One of the answers to it is the need for us to see our job as not just educating children, but educating the public, educating business community members, educating the political community, community-based organizations, and the like as to what kinds of strategies are most likely to help children. My experience is that leaders in the business community are increasingly open to learning from educators the kinds of strategies they might employ in order to support schools. Many are saying, We want to go beyond adopt-a-school programs. We don't want to tell you how to do your job; we want to find ways to support you in doing your job. As educators both individually and collectively, we need to offer responses and proposals to show them how they can support us in making the kinds of changes we all want. The receptivity among these groups is greater than it has probably ever been, and we must take advantage of that.

Q: Would you comment on the issue of time? I'm a second-grade teacher. I'm proud of my state, and I've been invited to help with policy decisions, but they're made on Wednesday. I was invited to participate in something I really believe in and want to help with, but finally I had to decline unless I could come on Saturday because I have 25 second graders. It takes two days to prepare for the one day I'm going to be gone. I'm out making policy decisions and helping and I'm asked to come back, but then the meeting is set on Wednesday. I would appreciate your comments, because I struggle, as many teachers do, with my responsibility to my 25 students versus to the state of Oregon.

Dr. Darling-Hammond: That's a great question, and what we do about time is the fundamental question of school reform. What I see as the most continuously successful solution to that problem is the move to organize schools around team teaching. Teachers need recognition of this full and complete professional role, so that such time away from school is regarded not as release time but as part of teaching work. A number of schools have begun this transformation to working in teams, so that when one member of the team is attending something outside of school, another is there working with children they are familiar with. This often is enhanced in professional development schools where interns are placed for their first year of teaching and there are several people working with the same group of students, sometimes even for more than one year. They may stay with that group of students for two or three years, which again makes it even easier to know how to work flexibly with the group. Having that team environment is a critical part of the solution.

But school time also needs to be restructured so that there is a reduction in the time that teachers are expected to be working with groups of students as opposed to working with their colleagues to improve the teaching and learning environment. This can be accomplished by means of block scheduling in which, for example, students meet three times a week for 70-minute periods instead of five times a week for 40-minute periods. Other strategies could also be employed, permitting substantial blocks of time for teachers to work together, whether within the school or outside it, where the professional work that you refer to has to be carried out.

Q: I'm a policy maker from Hawaii. In addressing the question of how to retain the best and the brightest in the classroom, our governor, in his state of the state address, noted that the further one moves away from the classroom along the career compensation ladder, the more money one makes. Would you comment on that please?

Dr. Darling-Hammond: The idea is that getting away from children makes an educator more important . . . Well, there are a lot of efforts being made to change that incentive structure. If teaching is to be a full profession in which knowledge of students and knowledge of good practice—and how to change practice—are merged (which, by the way, is how we're going to achieve the best policy making at the school and district levels), we have to rethink that incentive structure. There *have* been efforts to create the kind of career ladder that does not pull people out of the classroom in order to be acknowledged. The National Board for Professional Teaching Standards intends to transform that as well. Teachers who are committed to their teaching and committed to their professional work in schools should be able to both teach in the classroom *and* have the kind of remuneration necessary to send their own children to college without having to abandon the profession.

Q: I would like to applaud you for your vision of the schools of the future. But I have also seen immediate need for teachers in the classroom; and while most of us agree that alternative programs such as

Teach for America do not produce the kinds of teachers we need, I would like to know your view on how we might be able to use talents of veteran teachers to help produce them.

Dr. Darling-Hammond: One of the things that we need to do as professionals is bring bright, young, eager college graduates who want to commit to teaching and help design a preparation program that will *allow* them to be successful. What must be reversed is the situation in which committed people come in bright-eyed and bushy-tailed and leave within the first year of teaching. Part of the task, rooted at the local level, is to create supports for incoming teachers. We've worked, for example, in New York, at a number of universities to provide mentoring and continuing professional education for those kinds of recruits. We want to help them acquire the knowledge base for teaching through their work with mentors. In this way, their first few years will be well supervised; they will not be abandoned to the difficult and often brutal circumstances of the school system.

The other part of the task is to lobby for the re-creation at the federal level of the kind of programs that existed until 1980. The urban teacher corps, for example, and other kinds of recruitment and scholarship and forgivable loan programs for teachers can, in fact, underwrite the preparation of people who want to commit to teaching. Many of us were trained at a time when National Defense Student Loans were available, as was urban Teacher Corps Preparation. These were serious investments on the part of the federal government to support education in the national interest, and it's time to strengthen that kind of program again.

Q: I am an administrator from the state of Michigan, and I find myself very frustrated by the amount of time I have to give to incompetent teachers at the expense of students who have to sit there for nine months while I offer these services. I am looking for suggestions from you or from the legislature on how to help, because I think we're wasting a lot of valuable time.

Dr. Darling-Hammond: That's a very important question for the accountability of the profession. An effective approach to it that a number of districts have adopted—Toledo, Rochester, and Cincinnati come to mind—has teacher associations working in conjunction with the Board of Education to create a strategy for teacher evaluation that aims to ensure that every classroom has a teacher who really deserves to be there and who works well with children. In addition, teachers are serving as mentors to newcomers, and this is part of their evaluation for tenure. There are also programs in which teachers who are having serious difficulty can receive intensive assistance from a consulting teacher over the period of a year and in which the joint administrator and teacher committee managing the program decides whether the person ought to remain in the profession. In all of these cases there have been real results as teachers have become part of the process of designing and implementing a professional accountability system to ensure that every person who stands in front of children in the classroom truly deserves to be there.

8

School Reform: A Conversation with America's Educators

Valerie Mills

Milken Family Foundation National Educator Award recipients are poised to move from a decade of reports and dialogue into a period of planning and implementation. We have examined America's educational system from state, national, and international perspectives. We have looked at school subject areas and the various socioeconomic, political, and ethnic factors that affect schools. Research on the effective school has addressed every variable in the equation of how children learn. Educators have discussed and dissected these reports at conferences and colloquia. As the state of education has made newspaper headlines, best-seller lists, and the evening news, business leaders, politicians, and the general public have joined in the debate on school reform.

This chapter considers educators' dialogue as we take our first steps toward systemic change. And there *is* a subtle change in that dialogue. Discussion now centers on priorities among possible starting points for school reform. We are asking who should be involved, what our goals and responsibilities should be, and how we can meet our goals and sustain change over time. Finally, we are asking about the resources necessary to make a truly effective educational system a reality.

Implicit in the following discussion is the assumption that change must come to education and that *educators* will be at the center of that change. This chapter provides the reader with a "place at the table" as outstanding educators from across the country discuss the difficulties of implementing change in America's schools.

The 1992 Milken Family Foundation National Educator Award Retreat brought together nationally recognized educators representing every facet of American education. Following Chester E. Finn and Henry M. Levin's outlines of the various challenges of education reform, the

Award recipients met in small groups to discuss the speakers' views and their own ideas and experiences regarding school reform.

The discussion sessions were as lively and energized as one might expect from a roomful of teachers, administrators, and curriculum specialists dedicated to education and passionate about the needs of children. These educators didn't require a decade of dialogue to be convinced of the need to move our educational system into the twenty-first century, and they were more than eager to take on reform. Although the participants expressed views that were as diverse as the school settings in which they work, there was considerable agreement on many issues. Following is a synthesis of the ideas and reactions expressed during these sessions. The discussion is based on four topics: the need for a vision, reform participants and their responsibilities, school standards and their assessment, and the actual changing of schools and its implications.

The First Topic: Begin with a Vision

Before we begin to re-create education in American schools, as a nation of teachers, students, parents, businesspeople, and politicians, we need to agree on the mission of schools. Given the raft of reports on the shortcomings of American schools, and given the growing demands of a technology-based society, it is clear that schools need to change. The educators gathered for these discussions felt strongly that our first order of business must be to reach a consensus on the goals and responsibilities of our educational system. Pursuing a common vision is our best hope for developing a plan that will succeed in creating effective reform.

The Cheshire Cat tried to make this point in *Alice's Adventures in Wonderland*:

> "Would you tell me, please," said Alice, "which way I ought to walk from here?"
> "That depends a good deal on where you want to get to," said the Cat.
> "I don't much care where . . . ," said Alice.
> "Then it doesn't matter which way you walk," said the Cat.
> "so long as I get somewhere," Alice added as an explanation.
> "Oh, you're sure to do that," said the Cat, "if you only walk long enough."
> (Carroll, 1941)

Many of the educators gathered agreed with the Cat. In their local districts they had walked long enough to know they were "somewhere," but they didn't know where they ought to be. Though these educators have begun to develop a new vision in their schools, they warned that the process is not easy. It takes time, imagination, leadership, a willingness to take risks, and the energy to commit to yet more demands. Participants cautioned that educators must strive toward consensus in an environment defined by enormous diversity of culture and need.

There is concern among researchers that beginning the process of reforming schools by defining a vision is impossible, because teachers are locked into the picture of schools as they currently exist. Some researchers are afraid that educators will not be able to see beyond the present. As Sarason (1982) suggests, "existing regularities" can prevent educators from seeing the "universe of alternatives."

Discussion on this view prompted some teachers to point out that staff development opportunities are helpful in opening up the thinking of educators. In-service programs were also seen by many participants as a useful mechanism through which teams of educators can develop unity of purpose. Finally, educators with some expertise in this process suggested that the vision needed to begin effective reform does not have to be perfect, that it should be a work in progress. David (1991) points out that one of the features that distinguishes restructuring from previous reform efforts is that it is seen as a long-term commitment to fundamental, systemic change.

Traditionally, the effectiveness of education has been considered from the standpoint of the opportunities offered to students. Today, however, educators are shifting toward a paradigm that measures school quality according to what is learned by individual students. In his presentation, Finn described this paradigm shift as "a vast transformation of the very meaning of education," and participants in the small discussion groups agreed unanimously that the first order of business must be to reach a consensus on the goals of our educational system.

Lezotte and Jacoby (1990) challenge educators to consider two questions as they conjure a new vision for schools: What do we want our students to learn and be competent at? And, do we expect this knowledge from all or some students? Much of the discussion among participants and the guest speakers focused on one of these key questions.

Finn focused on the first question in citing President Bush's National Education Goals (U.S. Department of Education, 1991), and in drawing participants' attention to the need for unity of vision at the national level. Participants agreed that state and local schools would benefit from national standards that describe in global terms the knowledge and skills students will need to function successfully in the twenty-first century. Teachers were eager for this sort of guidance, particularly where it concerned content areas. Given the diversity of student populations, however, participants cautioned that specific student outcomes and the instruction to meet those outcomes need to be defined at levels closer to the classroom. Putting this need for variation at the local level aside momentarily, there was agreement that schools across the United States should be focused on a common broadly defined core of knowledge and skills that all students are expected to learn.

Levin addressed the question, "From which students do we expect this learning?" with particular attention to the fact that common goals be assigned to all students. His focus on the needs of at-risk students directed attention to the classroom. Currently, at-risk students are usually separated from the mainstream and assigned to remedial specialists. But to place at-risk students in remedial programs is to deny them access to the level of instruction available to mainstream students and to withhold opportunities and benefits attached to such instruction.

We also know that tracking is not effective. The work of Oakes (1985), Slavin (1987, 1990), George (1987), and Garmoran and Berends (1987) clearly shows that ability grouping does not improve student learning for either remedial students or gifted students. Tracking and remedial programs are evidence of the separate goals we currently establish for at-risk students. Retreat participants spoke eloquently of the need for an educational system that will serve the needs of at-risk and mainstream students equally. The vision and the goals we establish must apply to all students. Some educators questioned the expectation that schools will successfully educate all students. Edmonds (1979), in his research on effective schools, identified elementary schools where all students, disadvantaged or not, could be taught the skills needed to succeed in the next grade level. Edmonds concludes, "We can, whenever and wherever we choose, successfully teach all children whose schooling is of interest to us; . . . we already know more than we need to do that; . . . and whether or not we do it must finally depend on how we feel about the fact that we haven't so far." (p. 23)

A common vision of what we expect *every* student in the United States to learn is the first element of a plan that will afford educators the direction necessary to create productive, sustained, systemic change in our schools.

The Second Topic: Who Is at the Helm

There are a number of competing forces in the decision-making arena. Federal funding, for example, which is available for special education programs such as Chapter 1 for below-grade-level students, carries detailed requirements that allow little spending flexibility for local districts. In an effort to raise the minimum level of standards for all districts, some state governments are extending their reach to local areas of interest, such as state-written exit tests. Efforts such as these are narrowing the purview of local decision making. From this environment comes a chorus of demands that local schools and teachers be held accountable for what students learn or, more precisely, for what they do *not* learn in the classroom. In short, educators feel that those at the helm are holding the crew responsible for sailing the boat off the edge of the world.

While this sort of national and state intervention may be well-intentioned, all participants agreed that it is, in the final analysis, counterproductive. Levin stated, "If the school is to achieve its vision of educational success, administrators, teachers, other staff, parents, and students must participate in making informed decisions regarding school activities." With this, Finn concurred. And Retreat participants echoed their support for site-based management models in schools. Although eager to take on additional responsibilities, many participants cautioned that this aspect of school reform is complex. Time must be provided for all those involved to meet and review issues related to their new responsibilities. Parents, teachers, central office and building administrators, and school board members must adapt to new roles. Administrators have the particular challenge of finding a new and balanced kind of control. In general, those currently responsible for making decisions, whether at the local, state, or national level, need to be prepared to relinquish or share significant portions of that power. Participants commented that site-based management is most frequently seen in elementary schools, where staffs are relatively small and student needs less diverse. (Chicago schools, it should be noted, are a striking example of a system that has successfully introduced site-based management models at all levels.)

Finally, although there was agreement that important decisions regarding schools should be made at the classroom level, there was also agreement that attached to the authority to make decisions should be responsibility for the outcomes of those decisions. Thus, as decision-making power is transferred to the schools, a system designed to ensure accountability must also be put into place, so that in the end the crew *will* be held responsible for the ship's journey, but only after they have been given an opportunity to help chart their own course.

The answer to the question of who, in addition to education professionals, should be involved in educational decision making was *parents*. Finn pointed out that only 9 percent of a child's first 18 years is spent in school. Hence, "parents are the single most important influence in the [remaining] 91 percent [of children's lives]."

Participants agreed that the role of parents in schools must be expanded. They noted that parents need to help define and advance the mission of schools. The Retreat educators believe that when parents are considered to be a part of the process they are more likely to become involved. Further, when parents understand what schools are trying to do for their children they can more effectively support and reinforce the efforts of teachers and administrators at home. Parents thus significantly augment the crew, and, in giving them a stake in the bounty for which we sail, we capture their attention and inspire their goodwill.

The Retreat participants believe that schools, particularly high schools, need to build collaborative teams committed to educating students. Participants pointed out that it will not be enough simply to offer parents and other members of the community an opportunity to become involved. Schools need to find ways to *include* parents. Many participants cited examples of such programs, including grandparents' programs, parent handbooks, and after-dinner workshops such as the family math concept described by Stenmark, Thompson, and Cossey (1986). A number of detailed methods for establishing regular communication between home and school were discussed.

Research supports the view that parental involvement is a critical component of successful schools. Two of the three key ingredients that promote child development and learning in schools, as outlined by Yale's James Comer (1988) following his 12-year project to build effective schools from two troubled inner-city elementary schools in New Haven, focus on the need for parents to be active participants in schools. These key elements are involvement in school governance by parents (along with teachers, principals, mental health specialists, and nonprofessional support staff) and the active support of parents for school activities. Parental and community involvement in schools seems particularly important in reducing the impact of poverty on children. Barquet (1991) argues, "Once and for all, we must come to terms with the realization that in order to deal effectively with the issue of poverty (or any other form of institutionalized oppression) we must bring to the table all of those who are affected by it. . . . It is through meaningful participation and a sense of ownership on the part of those most affected that we increase the chances of success of any intervention." (p. 9) Levin expresses a similar view when he describes his accelerated schools as "crawling with parents." Both formal research and practical experience lead us to conclude that the parents are vital crew members on the ship that delivers opportunities.

An African proverb reminds us that "it takes the whole village to educate a child." Effective decision making in schools and instruction that produces the level of learning we want for all students will surely require the combined efforts of our "whole village."

The Third Topic: Establishing Standards

The focus now sharpens on educational standards. With the goals for education set, the task is to reach consensus on our expectations for student learning. At what level, then, should the standards be set: at the national, state, county/parish, or local level? How detailed should these standards be? For which areas of learning should standards be established? Who will measure progress toward these standards, and how? Retreat educators and speakers addressed each of these questions in some depth.

The issues of where standards should be set and how detailed they should be appear to be linked, for there is both a need for higher standards for all students and a need for teachers to design instruction to meet the particular needs of their students. An approach that accommodates both establishes standards that become broader the further one moves from the classroom. The National Education Goals enunciated by President Bush and the nation's governors in the spring of 1991 were deliberately cast in global terms. As Education Secretary Lamar Alexander (1991) pointed out: "There is an entirely appropriate concern that our strong American tradition of state responsibility for education and local control of schools be preserved and supported." (p. 5)

In and of themselves, the six National Education Goals can do little more than focus the nation's attention on key areas. Clearly, there is a need for greater specificity. There is also a belief that area specialists are the appropriate people to develop area standards or goals. The pioneering work done in school mathematics offers a good example of this approach. The mathematics education community, organized through the National Council of Teachers of Mathematics (NCTM), has developed a series of standards for mathematics curricula and evaluation against which local districts and states can judge their school programs. Designed to guide school mathematics reform over this decade, the framework is detailed enough to provide a unifying vision, yet not so specific as to prescribe a specific curriculum. The goal of its authors was to produce a document that could be used "as the basis for change so that the teaching and learning of mathematics in our schools is improved." (Working Groups of the Commission on Standards for School Mathematics of the NCTM, 1989, p. v) Direction such as this from the NCTM can provide the nation with a set of global guidelines that establish high standards while allowing state and local needs to be accommodated in the school and classroom.

This leaves the responsibility of setting more specific student performance outcomes at the state or local level, and many states are taking on this responsibility. Michigan, California, Maine, Connecticut, and Florida are a few of the states that have recently developed core curricula. Broader in scope than daily lists of instructional objectives but more specific than national education goals, these are intended to encourage greater consistency among district programs and to serve as the foundation upon which staff development and school improvement plans are designed. Some states' core curricula include the student outcomes on which proficiency tests are based. The results from these tests can be used to evaluate individual student performance as well as district and/or building performance. In some states, high school graduation is contingent upon "passing" these tests.

Independent of the role of various states, there is strong support for protecting the flexibility of local schools and classroom teachers. Speaking about effective schools, Edmonds (1979) notes that although teachers are working from an agreed-upon set of goals and expectations related to student achievement, "these schools recognize the need to modify curricular design, text selection, teaching strategy, and so on, in response to differences in family background among pupils in the school." (p. 22) Levin has shown that at-risk students in particular make greater gains when instruction capitalizes on existing student strengths. Such classroom adaptations would, at best, be difficult if national or state standards were too specific. The educators participating in the Retreat concurred with this thinking and added that there are additional benefits when specific outcomes are developed at the local or school level. Experience has taught them, for example, that a sense of involvement and commitment are valuable by-products of the process of determining student performance outcomes. Locally defined student outcomes also accommodate local diversity. And finally, there is a need to preserve a flexible school environment if we want to encourage excellence. Broad goals and instructional frameworks will be helpful, but decisions regarding classroom implementation of a standardized curriculum must be reserved for local districts and classroom teachers.

Regarding the areas of learning for which standards should be written, English, mathematics, science, history, and geography have traditionally led the list. Close behind are areas that address the use of technology and higher-order thinking skills, such as reasoning, critical thinking, and problem solving. Finn believes that our expectations should be limited to cognitive learning. In the small group discussions, however, many educators expressed the belief that goals from the affective domain are equally critical and should be specifically addressed in schools. They feel it is important to require outcomes that reflect community values, personal and civic responsibility, cooperative behavior in group settings, and an appreciation of learning as a lifelong process.

Many of these affective goals are essential to students' using information from the cognitive domain. It does little good to teach a child to do an electronic search, for example, if he or she is incapable of formulating relevant questions or understanding the importance of reliable information. Clearly, goals from both domains are necessary components of the core outcomes envisioned for well-educated students.

The fourth question is generally considered to be the key to successful implementation of new standards: How will progress toward these goals be measured, and by whom? There is an old saying that what is measured is valued and what is valued is measured. The first half of that adage can be viewed as gentle coercion, the second as a measure of commitment to explicit ends. It suggests that students required to demonstrate competence will be motivated to value the skills and knowledge that are assessed. Furthermore, school districts and communities that confront the challenges of implementing new standards must have accounting systems that will provide meaningful feedback if they are to fulfill the promise of change. If we do not insist on such feedback for students and for educators, then we cannot claim to be serious about achieving our goals.

Among educators gathered at the Retreat there was strong support for a comprehensive system of assessment and accountability, the two sides of the measurement coin. Educators repeatedly stressed the need for assessment instruments that will provide feedback on the full set of desired outcomes. While pencil-and-paper tests may be effective for assessing some skills, they are not sufficient for assessing others, particularly those in the affective domain. Performance tests, portfolios, long-term projects, and other instruments (some with technological enhancements) are needed to provide complete information about student knowledge and skills. A considerable number of states, schools, commercial testing companies, and even the National Assessment of Ed-ucational Progress (NAEP) are experimenting with a variety of these testing tools, and educators should have an attractive array of assessment instruments available in the next few years. Many of these authentic assessment forms cost more in both funding and time, but educators feel that if we are serious about *each* of the stated goals, we must be willing to invest in a complete, reliable information feedback system.

Although standards for criteria were not specifically addressed by either keynote speaker, participants noted that because instruction, assessment, and eventually accountability are linked to student out-comes, it is imperative that standards be accompanied by clearly de-fined, measurable criteria. Teachers must understand precisely what they need to teach, and students need to understand what they must learn. Standards at the level of assessment must be measurable.

The other side of the measurement coin is accountability—that is, incentive to meet high expectations. Education has always possessed a system of accountability, and its emblem is the diploma. In American education today, students are expected to collect credits toward graduation. Teachers and administrators report to their school boards the percentage of total student enrollment to whom diplomas are issued, and school boards pass the information on to the communities that elect them. As long as a school system issues a large number of diplomas, everyone is satisfied. As the vision and the goals of education shift, however, from process to product—that is, to well-educated students—the system that holds educators and students responsible must also change. Although "Carnegie units" may be useful for a system whose goal is providing students *access* to knowledge, they do not assure that students have acquired a specific level of learning in any given area. Nor do graduation statistics based on Carnegie units ensure that educators have taught students what we believe successful adults need to know.

Educators at the Retreat and elsewhere believe we need to change the current system of accountability both for school personnel and for students. Participants *did* agree on some aspects of this new system. First, they concurred that better incentives for students are needed. Student performance, particularly in high school, has little bearing on what students will do later. Finn pointed out in his presentation that few employers request high school transcripts, and only a handful of universities have truly rigorous entrance requirements. Universities and employers are demanding diplomas, and students are giving them exactly what is required; in the process, however, they are "just getting through" school. We need to replace the Carnegie unit system with one that provides evidence of student learning. We also need to convince businesses and institutions of higher learning to accept the new approach.

A second aspect of assessment and accountability upon which the Retreat participants focused was the impact of examination systems on minority and low-income students. Participants argued strongly that all students must have full access to the resources necessary for them to meet prevailing education standards. Emphasizing the need for a level playing field in schools, both for teachers and for students, educators cited as key sources preschool readiness, per pupil spending, access to technology, appropriate class size, sufficient textbooks and classroom materials, and well-trained teachers and administrators.

One aspect of accountability that remains unresolved is an appropriate reward system for teachers. Some educators feel that incentives should be directed toward individual teachers. Career ladders as well as pay scales calibrated to responsibility levels and student performance were cited as ways to ensure that goals are met. Levin, and others, suggested that such an accountability system be maintained at the institution level, with schools being recognized for their overall performance. If we are able to define the responsibilities at any given level of education, then it is appropriate to assess progress and to formulate a response at that level as well. This implies that rewards and remediation will be appropriately applied at the levels of both teacher and institution.

Finally, a caveat about rewards for teachers. Substantial evidence suggests that money may not be the most important incentive for educators. According to Glickman (1991), "Outstanding teachers do not teach for external incentives but for the pleasure of seeing the effects of their decision on students." (p. 6) He supports this position with quotations from the writings of educators who have been honored. Following is an excerpt from a book by one such teacher, Garret Keizer (1988):

> Last year my freshman student Jessica Davis took first prize of a thousand dollars in the Honors Competition for Excellence in Writing. I taught composition in Jessica's English class, and when we learned of her candidacy, I gave her extra coaching outside of class, which she graciously acknowledged in the newspaper articles about her. But the fact is, I did not make Jessica Davis a good writer. Somewhere on the scale of merit between me and God are at least eight elementary and middle school teachers. . . .
>
> As I write, one of our first grade teachers is adjusting the last hem of the authentic Pilgrim costumes she has sewn for every student in her class. A girl so poor that she has on occasion come to school without underwear stands smoothing down the folds of her long dress in wonderment. "See my dress!" she calls out to the visitor. It may be the cleanest, newest, handsomest thing she has ever worn—this garment of another age's austerity. How many hours this teacher must have spent at home behind a sewing machine—how many seconds will it take to punch her dedication into someone's business-model, performance-oriented, incentive-based computerized version of how schools ought to run. (pp. 117-119)

Such stories remind us that no single educator is responsible for any student's success and that good teachers do the right thing for the right child at the right time. Tomorrow's child will need something different, and the good teacher will be there to accommodate the new needs.

Considered from another perspective, it is also striking that teachers regularly spend their own money (an average of $250 per year) on teaching supplies. Among Milken Family Foundation National Educator Award recipients, the second most common use of the $25,000 that accompanies the Award (after putting the money into savings) is to put it toward students' needs. Give good teachers money, and they spend it on their students. An effective reward system for really good educators, then, is not as simple as paying them more for better student performance. Perhaps after we establish a salary scale that demonstrates respect (in Japan, teacher salaries rank in the top 15 percent nationally), we should consider offering educators incentives that make teaching children an easier task. Incentives such as opportunities to work with small groups on special projects, better work environments, and superior teaching resources should be included in a reward system. Student learning is its own reward for a good educator.

What happens when a teacher or school system fails to meet its goals? Participants in the Retreat's small group discussions addressed this side of the accountability question as well. Educators were anxious to say that reeducation, rather than sanctions, is an appropriate response. Suggestions for reeducation approaches included a system of peer review that would fit into a site-based management approach and a sys-tem of national boards, where standards for teaching would be defined in a way similar to those for student goals and objectives. An effective accountability system must nurture excellence, even as it refuses to tolerate ineffective educators. As Finn noted in his presentation, "An education system [exists] primarily for the benefit of its consumers, not its producers." Educators must be prepared to put the needs of students above those of educators when it can be demonstrated that educators are not meeting their responsibilities. Education professionals can begin by changing union practices that currently protect members who are not performing adequately.

The Fourth Topic: Changing Schools

Values, beliefs, and behaviors; time as a resource; well-directed research; school choice; the basic welfare needs of children that educators are expected to meet—these are the concerns of educators as they get down to the real business of changing schools. Each of these issues is directly associated with the restructuring of schools. Discussion of these issues provided some insight into the most pressing issues facing educators as we write the opening chapters of school reform in the 1990s.

One of the most challenging aspects of school reform will certainly be aligning educators' actions with their visions and goals. It is much simpler to describe a system to educate students than it is to change the behavior that will animate the system's values. A good example of this problem can be seen in tracking. If we truly believe it is our responsibility to impart a core of knowledge and skills to students, then we should ensure that our classrooms create effective learning environments. Tracking persists despite the fact that it does not improve learning for either gifted or remedial students. Even with research proof, convincing teachers to drop ability grouping is proving difficult, for behavior does not necessarily follow from what we know. New goals require doing things differently and taking risks; and taking risks means being prepared to fail before you succeed. Retreat educators voiced concern over these issues and emphasized that change will require a supportive environment for teachers and administrators.

In addition to the demands inherent in aligning values and behavior, there are other obstacles to reform. Finn pointed out that teachers, parents, students, and administrators all believe schools are in trouble everywhere but in their own districts. Changes that will affect student learning, however, must eventually occur at home, in the classroom.

Participants acknowledged the importance of inspiring a commitment to change among parents, students, school personnel, businesses, and local colleges and universities. The shared understanding within the school community of the need for change can be a decisive element in the success of school reform.

Most adults understand education in the terms in which they received it, and convincing them to rethink those terms is a prerequisite of meaningful change. Most adults learned that schooling and job training happen between the ages of 5 and 18 years, or slightly longer for those wanting a college degree. In a society in which the sum of knowledge is doubling every 10 years and in which the average person will have seven or eight different jobs in his or her adult working career, education must be a lifelong process. Schools must accommodate this change by providing all students with the skills to become independent learners. That means that the entire school community needs to alter its thinking about what schools should emphasize. Because this change in curriculum priorities will accompany a change in understanding about the role of schools, participants agreed that educators must be alert to the beliefs of the education community at large as we attempt to change the system.

An individual awareness of the problems facing schools, an ability to change beliefs and behavior, and an enduring commitment to change are essential to our mission. Each of these represents a formidable challenge; taken together, they give us an idea of the enormity of the task of restructuring schools.

Educational research is an underused assist to reform, and participants were eager to discuss instructional approaches that have shown promise in research classrooms. Thematic instruction, interdisciplinary courses, multimodal lessons, and heterogeneous grouping were among the instructional approaches discussed. Classroom time management, cultural variations in learning styles, the role of self-esteem, cooperative learning, and authentic assessment are just a few of the areas generating research literature. The relevance of such research projects underscores the importance of school systems' working with universities as well as with private sector organizations.

Time, our most precious resource, was also a focal point. The Retreat participants pointed out repeatedly that as responsibility for decision making and individual student learning is increasingly shifted to educators, time must also be provided for them to handle these additional responsibilities. Among the activities for which the educators noted they need more time are site-based management, incorporating research into school programs, participating in peer review activities, developing curricula that will support new content area guidelines, individual and collaborative faculty projects, working with parents and community members to implement new forms of assessment, and reviewing changes as they are implemented.

Mike Cohen, director of the National Center on Education and the Economy, recommends an intensive investment in professional development to accommodate the major change anticipated in the role of education professionals (Brandt, 1991). Experience from successful projects that have focused on a single content area also indicates that long-term staff development is a critical component of successful change. In a survey of school improvement programs, Joyce, Hirsh, and McKibbin (1983, 1991) note that inadequate attention to staff development is a significant factor in the failure of schools attempting substantive change by means of the curriculum. Further, Joyce, Murphy, Showers, and Murphy (1989) point out that those school improvement plans that have resulted in dramatic improvement in student learning paid attention to social dynamics and staff development. Deputy Secretary of Education David Kearns (1991) cites teacher training as "an essential aspect of improving today's schools." Educators in school classrooms, universities, private education foundations, and government agencies agree that educators need time apart from traditional responsibilities in order to make this new vision of schools a reality.

But where will this time come from? Educators do not believe that substantial amounts of time should be taken from student instruction. Instead, they suggest that many schools can restructure their school calendars to find time for adequate staff development. Retreat participants reported a variety of reorganized schedules, including shortened class periods, lengthened school days or school years, and year-round schooling with additional days for staff development. Schedules that accommodate both instructional and staff development needs are clearly an attainable and critical component of successful school restructuring.

Retreat participants agreed that a broader definition of the role of schools, including responsibilities other than teaching, must be addressed from the first day of restructuring. Although they indicated that they are frequently overwhelmed by the mounting needs of today's students, most expressed the opinion that schools can succeed only if they address these needs directly.

Ensuring that every child entering kindergarten is ready to learn is considered an essential part of the definition of school responsibility. Participants cited the investment—both human and financial—involved in communities' addressing children's needs *before* they fall behind in school. Four to five dollars in welfare and criminal justice are saved for every one dollar spent in early intervention programs such as Head Start. Students who have had the benefit of these programs, furthermore, are more likely to graduate from high school and to attend post-secondary institutions. Participants stressed the need for immediate full funding of Head Start programs.

Intervention programs that reach at-risk children at even younger ages—that is, at age 2 or 3 years—produce more dramatic results still. Projects such as the Carolina Abecedarian Project and New York's Mother-Child Home Program have reported steady increases in IQ scores for participating children. In addition to providing the stimulating environment that is critical for early childhood development, these projects also provide important human welfare supports, such as parent involvement programs, health and nutrition programs, and a range of other social services. Support in each of these areas contributes to the long-term well-being of students as well as to the creation of a level playing field for all children.

Unfortunately, many of the human welfare elements contributing to the success of preschool programs are generally absent from K-12 school programs. Although schools cannot be all things to all people, by coordinating with various social service agencies they can provide effective hubs for the delivery of vital services for students *and* their families. As Tasha Lebow (1991), field services specialist for the University of Michigan, writes, "Within poor communities schools are often a primary anchoring institution of positive activity and resource. Recognition of the school's stable relationship with the neighborhood and as a central point of contact for the family has led some schools to formally redefine their role in the community." (p. 24) Retreat educators concurred that, particularly in low-income communities, schools must directly address a broader spectrum of student and family needs.

Finally, the issue of choice—the selection by students and educators of the schools they would like to attend or work in—was addressed. All agreed that *every* child has the right to attend a good school and obtain a good education.

Proponents of choice argue that if disadvantaged children are entitled to attend good schools, we should let them *go* to good schools. A recent NBC television special on American schools highlighted one Carlos Perez, a Los Angeles high school student who is safe today because he was able to enroll at Hamilton High, a magnet school for students in the performing arts. Carlos believes that his being allowed to choose to attend Hamilton protected him from inevitable involvement in gang life.

Can we infer from the success of Carlos's experience that choice is the solution for all students? Educators at the Retreat voiced several caveats. First, they were concerned that choice might result in both racial and ethnic segregation, undoing much of the work of the civil rights movement over the past three decades. The choice of which school to attend might not be made simply on the basis of which school would help the student learn the most, but rather on the basis of racial or ethnic preferences. Participants also argued that when choice includes a voucher system that allows students to spend their tax dollars at schools outside their districts or out of the public school system entirely, scarce resources are drained from certain schools, forcing them into a downward spiral.

Retreat educators also questioned how particularly good schools would be able to accommodate all the students that might select them; they raised questions about transportation from distant districts; and they wondered if private schools would admit children if the amounts of their vouchers were less than the tuition. Choice offers a workable alternative only if these and other problems do not prevent students from attending the schools they choose. Educators at the Retreat were generally skeptical that proponents of choice can or will attend to all of these issues, and they feared for the children left behind in poor schools.

Choice does offer an immediate solution for some fortunate students, and it is the foundation for magnet schools, which provide outstanding resources for students from many districts and are highly successful at developing student excellence in specific areas of study. In these capacities, choice may be an important component in school reform. In and of itself, however, choice is only a salve on a diseased system. To the extent that it may lull some into a false sense of well-being, believing that a remedy has been found that does not require elaborate restructuring or substantive change, choice may actually interfere with long-term, broader treatment of America's educational ills. Choice does not directly cure education's ills, and its narrow focus does not encompass many of the problems inherent in our educational system. The Retreat participants concluded that as the sole prescription for ailing schools, choice is not sufficiently potent.

Conclusion

The 1992 Milken Family Foundation National Educator Awards Retreat brought together a group of educators who addressed nearly every current education reform. They called for a clear and unifying vision of education that will guide us into a new century of learning and embrace every child. They advanced a broader definition of the education community to include parents, business, and government. They recommended new education standards to encompass the range of skills and knowledge necessary in the "information age," and they suggested that the new measures should evaluate educational success according to outcome, not input and process. Finally, they discussed obstacles to the implementation of this new vision.

Retreat participants spoke urgently about current educational conditions and the need for innovative reforms, and they agreed that Americans' responses to the challenge of school reform may well constitute one of the most significant elements in our nation's well-being for the next century. The educators concluded that as individuals and as a nation, we must commit ourselves to creating an education system that equips every citizen with the tools to handle the many demands and contingencies of postindustrial life. Outstanding educators across the country are sorting out difficult issues and making important advances. As a nation, we must follow their lead on this vital journey.

9

The Practitioner: Creative Leadership and Impact

Linton Deck and Gordon M. Ambach

Here, two experts on creative leadership and state-level education management address the potential of the practitioner.

Creative Education Leadership

Some things really are more obvious than they may seem. Our social institutions, for example, are just a little bit out of whack. Take whatever institution you like. The family is different from the way it used to be, and the family is in trouble. Government as an institution is not what it ought to be, nor is the law, the church, schools, or any other institutions we might name. All of our social institutions are just a little bit not the way they ought to be, or not what we used to think they were. Of course, it is also more evident than it seems that we are in a time of fundamental change regarding the way we think about the world and ourselves as members of civilization. There has been a paradigm shift. We live in a time when the stories that we told ourselves and each other about how to understand the world and make sense out of our work and our relationship to each other are all shifting. And they are shifting *because* (and this is far more obvious than it seems, too) of the *success* of educational efforts in this country and across the world. Because we are better educated, we think differently about ourselves and about our world than we did heretofore. In the face of these changes, I believe it is more obvious than it seems that schools have to be *reinvented*, and that the reinvention must focus on the *future*.

To focus clearly on the future, it is helpful to think about the past, and in reviewing the history of our country, one can see that we have reinvented schools at least three times before. American schools began as *common schools*, a misnomer, for they were not common at all, if one takes *common* to mean available to everyone in the community. We had these so-called common schools until the Industrial Revolution, when, in response to that revolution and its imperatives, we reinvented the schools and made them into what might be called *factory schools*, or schools that sorted people according to the needs of an industrial economy. These factory schools Americanized immigrants.

In this century, we have again reinvented the schools, this time on the basis of public policy. These public priorities have generated unprecedented radical education policy in the United States. We know it as Public Law 94-142, and it has made schools *truly* common—that is, common to all the people. It has been appropriate public policy in my view, but it has led us to reinvent schools according to a hospital model, so that we speak of diagnosing educational needs and prescriptions to fill those needs.

Over the generations, then, we have reinvented our schools three times. Now it is time to do it again. Consider the following passage from Patricia Graham's *S.O.S.: Sustain Our Schools* (1992):

> Many Americans reminisce fondly about a golden age of American education. They long for a time when children were obedient, when city strife was at a minimum, when academic achievement was universal among those for whom society was concerned. And the institutions responsible for the golden age were the schools. Today much of the longing to return to the mythic golden age comes from the perceived decline in academic achievement among American high school students. Much of the current debate about educational reform in the United States focuses on the need for higher levels of academic achievement among higher percentages of American youth. The role of schools in effecting that transformation is central. Some critics mistakenly argue that the schools alone are causes of the academic inadequacies of the American youth. Schools indeed do bear part of that culpability, but they share it with others: families whose interest in their children's athletic prowess is greater than the interest in their studies; employers who hire teenagers for dead end jobs for 20 or more hours a week during the school year; communities that pay their able and effective teachers $25,000 annually and expect them to remain in teaching. In short, everybody has a responsibility for the current shortcomings in academic achievement and for creating the conditions that will make better education for everybody not just a slogan but a reality. (p. 16)

In other words, it isn't our fault that schools need to be reinvented, but it is our responsibility to do something about it.

So let's imagine a school—a school in which every teacher is an inventor of work, every student is a creator of knowledge, every classroom is a learning laboratory. And in this school, teachers design the laboratory, furnish it with materials, and guide the activities that engage students. And through this engagement, this work, students solve problems and create knowledge. They learn, and they learn how to learn.

Most of us, probably all of us, can imagine such a place—a place where every student succeeds. And most of us believe that schools *can* become such places—places where every teacher is a leader, every leader is a teacher, and every student is a success. How can we make such schools a reality? The question could not be put to a more appropriate group. The educational leaders we celebrate at this Retreat are the people who must reinvent the schools. Let us consider how this might work.

In education, as in any enterprise, change cannot begin until the leaders know what direction to take. That is why every journey toward school reinvention or restructuring begins with three essential questions: What is the *purpose* of the school? Who are the school's *customers*? How *well* does the school *serve* its customers? The answers to these questions can provide a very clear vision for schools to follow as they create an environment supportive of change and the achievement of goals. A vision of restructured schools is built on beliefs and values held by the leaders who have responsibility for the organization.

Let's briefly consider some of those beliefs. The primary purpose of schools, for example, is to create meaningful activities for their customers, their students. And schools must engage those customers in the activities created. A second belief that would contribute to such a vision is that every student can and will learn, given the right opportunities. A third belief is related to learning opportunities determined by the nature of the activity in which students engage. That activity is best called *knowledge work*. For such beliefs and values, for such a vision for schools and schooling to become a reality, the organization must have the capacity to pursue essential strategies for reinvention.

From a systems perspective, there are at least seven strategic imperatives for organizational reinvention (see Center for Creative Leadership, 1992). Let's review them briefly. The first strategic imperative is a *shared vision* among the leaders and the followers. The second is *participatory leadership*—that is, the undertaking of leadership roles in ways that do not occur in many human organizations now. The third is *management by results*, or management designed to assure positive results. A fourth imperative comprises the dual activities of *innovation and improvement*. Fifth are *continuity and institutionalization*—the ability to maintain the organization while institutionalizing new forms of relationships, new rules, and new roles for the people who make up the organization. The sixth requisite is *flexibility*—continually nurtured to permit improvement and constructive change. Finally, the seventh imperative is strong *appropriate support* from the body politic to allow for these changes.

I will focus on the first and most important of these, for if there is to be creative leadership within the school, it must be based on a shared vision. Any organization that wishes to begin a process of fundamental improvement and change must determine what the members of the organization believe about the organization's purpose. There must be identified a vision of what the organization will look like when that determination is realized. The vision should provide a structure of rules, roles, and relationships (the three Rs) appropriate to the accomplishment of the new purpose. Once the vision has been articulated, the school system or the local school can develop and implement strategies to help ensure that the vision is shared by the community.

Each of us has a vision, at least an unexpressed vision, of what schools should be—one may be illustrated by this anecdote from Roland Barth (1990). Some years ago he was rummaging around in rural Maine, and he came across a newspaper advertisement for used farm equipment. This is what the ad said: "For Sale, Model 95 International Harvester Haybaler. $900 as is. Working, but could work better." That is the way we might conceive of the desirable school: one that is working, but could work better.

The question, then, is, What is *your* vision of a good school? What are the images that a teacher, principal, librarian, or someone responsible for a special program hopes to see? Every practitioner's personal vision must be revealed and honored. Such visions are usually deep-seated but also sometimes fragmentary and not so well articulated. There are important reasons to discover and honor them, however; among other things, it is the practitioner's vision that contains prescriptions for school reform and reinvention that have the best chance to be taken seriously and enacted. They have the best chance to be upheld by the people whose responsibility they are.

There's a second reason educators should cultivate a vision of the schools they desire: Their vision is the product of years of experience and practice. Anyone who works in a school for 180 or 190 days a year, year after year, develops great practical knowledge about curriculum, child development, discipline, leadership, desegregation, parent involvement, and a host of other issues. Educators' insights, culled from years of experience, give richness and credibility to their vision of good education and good schooling.

Here is a vision of schools of the future to compare with your own vision:

> Schools should be places where every student is a consumer of "knowledge work"—that intellectual activity through which students learn skills

> and concepts and attitudes and ideas and procedures that are valued in a global, information-based economy. (Barth, pp. 129-130)

Schools must be places where every teacher is a leader and an inventor of knowledge work. Teachers are successful when students are successful at those tasks that develop valued skills and understanding.

A clear vision on the part of leaders of schools *can* make the decisive difference for the reinvention and restructuring of the schools in our communities, states, and nation. The vision of the educator is vitally important.

LD

Practitioner Impact at the State Level

We are living in a time of intense criticism of American education. We all feel it very deeply. It comes at a time when there are attacks on virtually all of our institutions, both public and private. These attacks express dissatisfaction with the fact that, at both national and institutional levels, we are not doing what we might. We are not meeting our expectations, either for ourselves or for our society.

Why is education under particular attack? The current disappointment and criticism have arisen, in part, because of the relatively recent widespread exposure of performance levels in education, because of increased testing and discussion of results, and, perhaps most important, because there have been well-publicized international comparisons made. These comparisons have not been confined to education. We see them in business and generally where self-containment has been lifted and we are looking at ourselves against the backdrop of economic competitors. International comparisons have led to a great deal of criticism of what we are doing in the schools, but I believe they can also be beneficial, providing we do not let them grind us down. We must turn the critics' energy toward issues that challenge our children, and indeed all of us, in the coming century.

Let us consider this challenge by first focusing on the importance of the teacher's voice. I have enormous faith in the energy and power of teachers across this country to improve the practice of our education system. There are abundant examples—successful projects in which I am sure many of the Retreat's participants have been involved—but the problem is a pattern of practice. How do we make universal what we know can be done well in one location or another? Indeed, how do we disseminate it within a single school district, let alone a state?

Wisdom comes from learning. It comes from educators and from researchers in business and industry who know what issues are key to the success of those enterprises. People at all levels of the educational system must share a common goal and must work to share successful practices if they are to accomplish that goal. The issue is not vertical but horizontal. The issue is whether there are shared strategies and a shared goal, and educators' part in developing these is absolutely critical.

At present, the reform efforts in this country are primarily focused on the classroom, and on the practice of teaching and learning. If one reviews the reform issues of the past three decades, one sees a focus on issues of finance, integration, desegregation, school organization, consolidation, and systems control. The focus has been on issues of licensure, on bargaining, on terms and conditions of employment. But today, the focus is increasingly on content and pedagogy—on what happens, if you will, when the teacher closes the door. For this reason, it is all the more important for the educator's voice to be heard.

If our systems are to be changed, we must understand all their constituent parts; we must understand where the leverage points are and how they can be used most constructively. One cannot isolate issues of curriculum or materials or staff development or learning technologies or conditions of practice or student motivation. They must be seen as a whole.

The orientation of educators toward students and the classroom is absolutely essential for policy making at the state level. On the issues of teaching and learning, the educator's voice carries a comparative advantage. But keep in mind, when one is advising at the state level, one is advising on large-scale systems where there may be hundreds of thousands or millions of students, and tens of thousands of teachers.

Even cloning the hundreds of outstanding teachers attending this Retreat would be useless unless we also developed a system that would organize outstanding educators so that their talents can be used. This is where the matter of extrapolating from individual classroom experience or school practice to larger systems becomes so important.

Let us now turn to the issue of state education policy, the fundamental authority for education. There is currently an interesting phenomenon in this country as we are both nationalizing educational issues and decentralizing educational decision making. Though it seems a contradiction in terms, the fact of the matter is that neither will be effective unless there is substantial attention given to the middle—that is, to state policy making.

Let us consider school-site decision making. The key decisions on school site issues made at the state level, incidentally, have to do with the kinds of decisions that should be made at the school-site level. If those decisions focus on the curriculum and on teaching practice, they make good sense. If those decisions are another version of the decisions made by school boards at the school district level, they probably won't make much difference. The question then is, How does the state form school-site decision-making processes, and what decisions should be made at the school level?

Regarding national aspects of education in this country, one sees a trend toward national goals, standards, and testing—a real turnaround, with polls now showing a considerable percentage favoring national goals and standards. This shift has to do with international competition, as we do not work in the international context state by state, but as a nation. In many respects, we already have a de facto national curriculum. Hence, if there are to be effective reform measures, the thinking is that they might as well be undertaken in a consolidated way, rather than 50 times over.

Another nationalizing pressure derives from the conjunction of education, health, and social services. Health, social services, and child-care policy in this country is predominantly set at the federal level. The more we link education policy to policy in these other areas, the more these decisions will be considered national.

There is an analogy here with the experience of the aerobics class or the exercise room: If you want to strengthen the extremities, you work on the middle. The kinds of decisions coming from the middle shape what happens, whether at the national or at the local level.

Finally, regarding the reasons for paying attention to state education policy: It is important to keep in mind that the more research and understanding we have about the comparative advantages of using different teaching strategies, materials, or content, the greater the likelihood that decision makers outside the classroom at the local, district, or state level will make decisions about them. This is particularly true at the state level. If such decisions are to be made, it is imperative that educators' voices be heard.

A useful exercise for educational practitioners is to imagine themselves in the role of state chief, and to ask, What would I do next week if it were my responsibility to improve education in my state? There are many approaches one can take to this imagined role. One might consider, for example, strategies surrounding the state aid for schools formula, or the issue of whether public funds should be used for private schools, or the best kind of strategy for dealing with school district organization.

A recent article by Mike Smith, dean of the School of Education at Stanford, and Jennifer O'Day (1992) has a good starting point in its focus on the systemic structure of schools and power at the state level for the purpose of organizing the talents, curricula, frameworks, standards, assessments, professional development, and accountability system into an improved school system.

Let's focus, for a moment, on the question of curriculum frameworks and assessments. Across the United States, at both national and state levels, there is intensified attention being paid to the design of curriculum frameworks and the establishment of standards, because it is in these area that general rules and codification are established, particularly regarding such issues as the control of content issues. When we consider such questions in terms of the individual, that is one thing; when we think about them among faculty, it is another, because what is happening in various classes or grade levels is very important to what happens in one's classroom, and a shared expectation of learning at different levels is absolutely critical.

The issue is, really, how educators would write state content standards. Would they approach the task as one of writing content standards for learning or for teaching? Would they include particular forms of pedagogy, such as specifications for accelerated learning, cooperative learning, or competitive learning? Or should that be done at a different level? And if it is done at a different level, what about the issue of whether pedagogical form is properly the domain of school district or individual school standards?

Let's consider assessments for a moment. From the teacher's perspective, the question, I believe, is this: Do state student assessments provide incentive for teachers to improve their practice? If they don't, what would a teacher in the role of chief school officer do to change the assessment, testing, or examination practice to assure a positive outcome?

Now, let's turn to avenues of influence for educators. First, one must analyze the substance of the case one is arguing. That is essential. Second, one must deal with the procedures.

There are many decision makers at the state level. They include, of course, chiefs and state board members, governors and state legislators. Increasingly, they include blue-ribbon panels, as well as business and other groups established to craft state reform packages. The educator's task is to assess very carefully the point of leverage in his or her own state. Even among state boards or chiefs, there are substantial differences in the power they have, their legal authority, and their influence. Generally, educators must put themselves in the position of those people to understand what decisions they can make and in what contexts they make them. They are not necessarily thinking about the same issues as practitioners. Timing, of course, is also extremely important. One needs to determine carefully when and where to deploy one's energies.

That said, there are two ways in which today's educators can exercise some very important influence: as individuals or as part of a corporate force. One of the most influential forms of representation an educator can have is through a school team or program, as part of a combined effort. This will likely be at a programmatic or school level rather than at the district level, because it is at that level that an individual teacher is part of a team, along with supervisors and principals. That is an important level at which to get across a message.

When I was commissioner of education for the state of New York, I had 22 advisory committees, an experience that convinces me educators should not confine themselves to committees made up only of teachers. More and more, advisory groups, committees, and blue-ribbon panels represent diverse interests. Educators need to inform themselves regarding just what committees exist and how they can be part of them. Needless to say, it is also crucial that they know about and work to shape the direction of teacher organizations and unions.

Finally, educators must keep sight of the issues that influence them, and must translate that knowledge into actions that can influence others. And in doing so, educators should always remember to keep their highest ideals. Such ideals can carry them through the roughest of times.

In closing, I would like to quote Daniel Webster (1964) on the timeless importance of education. "If we work upon marble it will perish," he wrote, "if we work upon brass, time will efface it; if we rear temples, they will crumble into dust; but if we work upon immortal minds, if we imbue them with principles, with just the fear of God, and love of our fellow-men, we engrave on those tablets something which will brighten all eternity" (quoted in Hurd, p. 70).

GMA

10

Improving America's Schools: A Call to Leadership

Cheryl L. Fagnano

The primary focus of the 1992 Milken Family Foundation National Educator Awards Retreat was the link between educational excellence and educational leadership. The Retreat's fundamental lesson was that practitioner leadership is the key to education reform. This concluding chapter joins that focus and lesson by providing a synopsis of Retreat participants' views, especially on the topic of *improving American education,* as well as offering an analytic profile of recipients of the Milken Family Foundation National Educator Award.

Retreat keynoters provided contrasting perspectives on American education and education reform. Chester Finn characterized American education as trouble filled and apparently impervious to reform efforts, pointing out that 10 years of blue-ribbon panels and reform reports, of intensive educational research and experimentation, of policy recommendations and legislative action have yielded little educational im-provement. Academically, American students continue to lag behind their counterparts in other industrialized nations, he noted. Dropout rates remain high for all, and especially high for African-American and Latino students, and colleges, universities, and employers continue to lament the lack of preparation of high school graduates.

Despite the reform movement's shortcomings, the past decade's research has yielded some important findings. Linda Darling-Hammond pointed out that a good deal more is now known about schooling, learning, and instruction than ever before. We know, for example, that educational excellence tends to languish in the general and flourish in the particular. We know that children and adults learn best when what they are taught is grounded in what they already know. We know that children do not learn what they are not taught. Thus, teachers who concentrate on providing a curriculum rich in meaning and complexity seem to be more successful than teachers who depend on drill and practice, worksheets, and rote learning. We know that when teachers and principals have a common vision of what students should learn in school they are more likely to achieve success. Indeed, according to Dr. Darling-Hammond, it would appear that much of the substance of educational reform has been formulated and is simply awaiting widespread implementation.

In fact, both Henry Levin and Linda Darling-Hammond cited compelling examples of schools and educational processes that are implementing what are considered among the best reform movements ideas. Dr. Levin pointed to his own work with accelerated schools for at-risk, underachieving students. These schools have undertaken serious initiatives to restructure, both systemically and pedagogically, and they are achieving remarkable success with students who are all too often written off by the education system. Dr. Darling-Hammond discussed the work in a number of New York City schools to bring whole-language instruction to the classroom and to develop effective strategies for working with students with limited proficiency in speaking English.

Retreat speakers illuminated at least three important realities of American education. First, there are serious problems; second, solid technical information exists to help solve these problems; and third, in schools and classrooms around the country these problems are being addressed effectively. The question then arises: How do we extend the use of solutions *known* to work? The unanimous answer among Retreat participants was to promote strong professional leadership within the classroom, the school, and the district. Indeed, most agreed that without such leadership the hard-won systemic and pedagogical lessons of the past decade will not be put to use. If our children are to achieve more, to learn more, and to acquire the intellectual tools needed to compete in a global economy, it will be because their individual teachers and principals led the way. To paraphrase Chester Finn, when actual people actually change their actual behavior, there is every reason to assume that our schools will improve. The Milken Family Foundation National Educator Award recipients are those actual people.

Researchers develop theories and methods for educational improvement, policy makers propose plans and solutions, and politicians write them into law. Ultimately, however, school principals and classroom teachers are the ones who make the changes necessary to ensure education reform. These men and women are America's true education leaders, and a detailed survey undertaken by the Milken Institute for Job & Capital Formation provides instructive data on the characteristics, career trajectories, and ongoing professional contributions of an outstanding group of them.

Recipients of the Awards constitute an educational group like no other in the United States and perhaps in the world. Although not formally chartered, this group of educators represents every quadrant of the country and constitutes one of the most interesting and potentially influential assemblies of educators in America today. Because their selection is based on one criterion—outstanding achievement—these men and women represent only one interest: the pursuit of excellence.

Initiated in California by Michael and Lowell Milken, the Milken Family Foundation National Educator Award is offered to professional educators in elementary, middle, and secondary schools. The Award has two primary purposes: to recognize, celebrate, and reward educators who make significant contributions to the education of children; and to heighten public recognition and appreciation of the teaching profession and thereby encourage talented men and women to enter the field of education.

In 1991, there were 312 Award recipients; in 1992 an additional 120 joined their ranks; and in 1993, 138 Award recipients from 25 states will join the group (Fagnano, 1993). Each is chosen because he or she has made a significant contribution to the development of innovative education programs and has demonstrated unusual ability to motivate students. In the case of administrators, the award is given for demonstrated success in attracting, supporting, and motivating committed teachers. Each recipient has a history of dedication to education.

In a Milken Family Foundation survey designed to provide a descriptive analysis of this singular group of educators, questionnaires were sent to all Award recipients. There was a 96 percent rate of response (Fagnano, 1993). Respondents fall into four categories: teachers (239), principals (108), administrators (28), other educators (33), and retired educators (4). Survey questions covered the areas of general demographics, educational background, professional activities and interests, school or district demographics, professional opinions, and nonprofessional activities. Following is a composite profile of this unique group.

Recipients graduated from high school in nearly every state in the nation. They range in age from 29 to 78, with an average age of 48. They are a diverse group, with an ethnic distribution similar to that of the United States as a whole: 14 percent African-American, 7 percent Asian-American, 72 percent Caucasian, 4 percent Latino, and 3 percent representing other ethnic groups. Historically, the education profession has been a ladder for upward mobility in our society (Lortie, 1975), and this has been the case for the Award recipients, as well. Like many of their counterparts in the education profession, the Award recipients tend to come from working class backgrounds (43 percent). However, virtually all currently identify themselves today as middle-class, with 27 percent categorizing themselves as upper-middle-class or wealthy.

Like the vast majority of students in the United States, Award recipients are products of the American public school system. A total of 88 percent graduated from public high schools, and the balance graduated from parochial or private independent schools. Not surprisingly, Award recipients are a highly educated group: 80 percent have master's degrees and 14 percent hold doctorates. Further, 75 percent received competitive academic awards as undergraduates, and 21 percent of those who attended graduate school received at least one academic award while there. A large majority (78 percent) achieved a 3.0 or better grade point average in college. Although eventually all became professional educators, only 38 percent graduated from college with degrees in education. As undergraduates, 16 percent majored in math or science, 20 percent in the humanities, 16 percent in social science, and 10 percent in other fields.

The expertise of Milken Family Foundation National Educator Award recipients extends to nearly every facet of education. Indeed, there are few areas of educational innovation, reform, and improvement to which these men and women have not contributed. The range of services these educators offer their students provides a prime example of their ingenuity and commitment. Schools today shoulder an increasing share of responsibilities that are external to education, and many educators have developed creative responses to these needs.

One Michigan Award recipient, for instance, has established an alternative school for teenage mothers. The students—who range in age from 10 to 18—not only have the chance to study academic and vocational subjects, but can be active, responsible parents to their children who are looked after during school hours in the school's nursery. Among the many other cases of highly effective, nontraditional services is that created by a California teacher whose music and dance program in a coeducational probation facility has transformed the self-perception and achievement levels of scores of young wards of the court.

Award recipients also have demonstrated both ingenuity and expertise in the area of curriculum development across the disciplines. An Oregon math teacher, for instance, trains teachers across the state to teach math as a lab course in which students collect data by computer and conduct analyses with statistical packages and spreadsheets. A science teacher from California engages the intellectual interest and personal involvement of high school students by taking them to local elementary and middle schools to *teach* what they have learned about everything from the dissection of a fetal pig to the transformation of energy.

Award recipients are in the forefront of developing inventive and effective methods of student and teacher evaluation. One Oregon math teacher has developed a student portfolio assessment technique that not only encourages students to evaluate their own work on a quarterly basis but also encourages the teachers these students will have the following year to make use of these data and techniques. The evaluation of teachers, of course, is equally fundamental to sound education, and one Colorado principal's novel approach is to involve teachers fully in all teachers' evaluation processes, giving them an active stake in their collective professional growth.

Milken Family Foundation National Educator Award recipients are also making important contributions in the area of school restructuring and school-site reform. One elementary school principal, for example, who used her Award purse to win matching grants from one private company and two state-funded programs, has transformed her school into a model of comprehensive and preventive social service delivery, providing everything from health checkups and child care to drug abuse prevention and employment referrals. This educator also plans to organize her school as one of Los Angeles's first Charter Schools, enabling it to operate independently of the parent district.

A number of Award recipients are literally extending the reach of their schools by means of technological innovations. In West Virginia, one English teacher has made long-distance interactive learning the order of the day; he linked his county's four high schools and the local community college by means of fiber-optic lines to which he gained free access, as well as via video communications and switching capabilities.

The 312 educators brought together for the 1992 Milken Family Foundation National Educator Awards Retreat constitute a unique and vital professional network spanning every part of the country. The combined expertise of this assembly covers the range of education concerns, allowing these individuals to make important contributions to one another's understanding of the profession and to the development of their mutual potential. High-quality education is imperative for the security of the individual, the community, and the nation. As committed providers of that education, the recipients of the Milken Family Foundation National Educator Award are an invaluable resource.

Note

1. In the 1950s, 1960s, and 1970s, when most of the Award recipients would have been attending high school, the nonpublic high school enrollment was 10.5, 10.9, and 9.1 percent, respectively, according to the U.S. Department of Education. (1988, p. 60, Table 44)

Bibliography

Aikin, W. M. (1942). *The story of the eight-year study, with conclusions and recommendations*. New York: Harper & Brothers.

Alexander, L. (1991, November 25). Toward world class standards. *Business Week*, p. 5.

Barquet, N. (1991, Summer). Unheard voices: A national origin perspective on the politics of poverty. *Equity Coalition for Race, Gender, and National Origin*, pp. 7-9.

Barth, R. (1990). *Improving schools from within: Teachers, parents, and principals can make the difference*. San Francisco: Jossey-Bass.

Birch, D. L. (1987). *Job creation in America: How our smallest companies put the most people to work*. New York: Free Press.

Bishop, J. (1992). Why U.S. students need incentives to learn. *Educational Leadership, 49*(6), 15-18.

Brandt, R. (1991, May). On restructuring schools: A conversation with Mike Cohen. *Educational Leadership, 48*, 54-58.

Cannell, J. (1989). *How public educators cheat on standardized achievement tests: The "Lake Wobegon" report*. Albuquerque, NM: Friends for Education.

Carroll, L. (1941). *Alice's adventures in Wonderland*. New York: Heritage.

Center for Creative Leadership. (1992). *Center for Creative Leadership*. Carrboro, NC.

Chamberlain, C. D. (1942). *Did they succeed in college? The follow-up study of the graduates of the thirty schools*. New York: Harper and Brothers.

Children's Defense Fund. (1991). *The state of America's children 1991*. Washington, DC.

Chubb, J., and Moe, T. (1990). *Politics, markets, and America's schools*. Washington, DC: Brookings Institution.

Coleman, J., and Hoffer, T. (1987). *Public and private high schools: The impact of communities*. New York: Basic Books.

Comer, J. (1988, November). Educating poor minority children. *Scientific American*, pp. 42-48.

Committee for Economic Development. (1991). *An assessment of American education: The view of employers, higher educators, the public, recent students and their parents* (Research Report No. 912061). New York: Louis Harris and Associates.

Council of Economic Advisers. (1992). *Economic report of the president*. Washington, DC: U.S. Government Printing Office.

David, J. L. (1991, May). What it takes to restructure education. *Educational Leadership, 48*, 11-15.

Dunn, L. (1992). [High-yield financing: Time series]. Unpublished raw data.

Edmonds, R. (1979, October). Effective schools for the urban poor. *Educational Leadership, 37*, 15-24.

Educational Testing Service. (1991). *The state of mathematics achievement: Executive summary: NAEP's 1990 assessment of the states.* Washington, DC.

Elam, S. M. (1992). The 23rd annual Gallup poll on the public's attitude toward the public schools. *Phi Delta Kappan, 73,* 1: 841-856.

Elam, S. M., Rose, L. C., and Gallup, A. M. (1991). The 22nd annual Gallup poll on the public's attitude toward the public schools. *Phi Delta Kappan, 72,* 1: 41-55.

Elam, S. M., and Gallup, A. M. (1989). The 21st annual Gallup poll on the public's attitude toward the public schools. *Phi Delta Kappan, 71,* 1: 41-54.

Employment and Earnings. (1992). Employees on nonfarm payrolls by major industry, 1941 to date. Vol. 39(12).

Fagnano, C. L. (1993). [Milken Family Foundation National Educator Award Recipients' survey: Awardee's employment position, state from which awardee graduated high school, age of awardee, ethnicity of awardee, other awards and honors of awardee]. Unpublished raw data.

Feldhusen, J. F. (1992). *Talent Identification and Development in Education (TIDE).* Sarasota, FL: Center for Creative Learning.

Feistritzer, C. E., Quelle, F., and Bloom, I. (1988). *Profile of school administrators in the U.S.* Washington, DC: National Center for Educational Information.

Fortune. (1981a, May 4). The 500 largest industrial corporations.

Fortune. (1981b, July 13). The Fortune directory of the 50 largest commercial banking institutions, life insurance institutions, diversified financial institutions, retailing companies, transportation companies, and utility companies.

Fortune. (1991a, April 22). The 500 largest industrial corporations.

Fortune. (1991b, June 3). The 500 largest service corporations.

Friedman, M. (1962). *Capitalism and freedom.* Chicago: University of Chicago Press.

Gardner, H. (1983). *Frames of mind: The theory of multiple intelligences.* New York: Basic Books.

Garmoran, A., and Berends, M. (1987). The efforts of stratification in secondary schools. *Review of Educational Research, 57,* 415-435.

George, P.S. (1987). *What's the truth about tracking and ability grouping really???* Gainesville, FL: Teacher Education Resource.

Glickman, C. (1991, May). Pretending not to know what we know. *Educational Leadership, 48,* 4-10.

Graham, P. (1992). *S.O.S.: Sustain our schools.* New York: Hill and Wang.

Hurd, C. (comp.). (1964). *A treasury of great American quotations: Our country's life and history in the thoughts of its men and women.* New York: Hawthorn.

Impact II. (1991). *The teachers' vision of the future of education: A challenge to the nation.* Mechanicsburg, PA.

Johnson, E. G. (1992). *The NAEP technical report.* (Research Report No. 21-TR-20). Washington, DC: Educational Testing Service.

Joyce, B., Hirsh, R., and McKibbin, M. (1983). *The structure of school improvement.* White Plains, NY: Longman.

Joyce, B., Hirsh, R., and McKibbin, M. (1991). *The structure of school improvement* (2nd ed). Aptos, CA: Booksend.

Joyce, B., Murphy, C., Showers, B., and Murphy, J. (1989, March). School renewal as cultural change. *Educational Leadership, 47,* 70-77.

Kearns, D. (1991, November 25). The business of business is also education. *Business Week*, p. 80.

Keizer, G. (1988). *No place but here: A teacher's vocation in a rural community.* New York: Viking Penguin.

Knapp, M. S., Shield, P. M., and Turnbull, B. J., (1992). *Academic challenge for the children of poverty* (Vols. 1-2). Washington, DC: U.S. Department of Education, Office of Policy and Planning.

Lacey, D. (1992, January/February). Permanent staff cutting has continued into 1992 at a brisk pace. *Workplace Trends*, pp. 1-2.

Lapointe, A., et al. (1992). *Learning mathematics.* Princeton, NJ: Educational Testing Service, Center for the Assessment of Educational Progress. (ERIC Document Reproduction Service No. ED 347 081)

Lebow, T. (1991, Summer). Pieces of the puzzle: Programs from which we can learn. *Equity Coalition for Race, Gender, and National Origin*, pp. 22-27.

Levin, H. M. (1988). *Accelerated schools for at-risk students.* New Brunswick, NJ: Center for Policy Research in Education.

Levin, H. M. (1991). Local knowledge, academic skills, and individual productivity—an alternative view. *Education Policy, 5*, 4: 341-342.

Levin, H. M. (1986). *Educational reform for disadvantaged students: An emerging crisis.* West Haven, CT: National Education Association Professional Library.

Levin, H. M. (1992). Educational acceleration for at-risk students. In A. C. Huston (Ed.), *Children in poverty.* New York: Cambridge University Press.

Lezotte, L. W., and Jacoby, B. C. (1990). *A guide to the school improvement process based on effective school research.* Lansing: Michigan Institute for Educational Management.

Lortie, D. (1975). *Schoolteacher: A sociological study.* Chicago: University of Chicago Press.

Louis Harris and Associates. (1992). *New teachers, part I-III* (Research Report Nos. 922021-922023). New York.

McCarthy, J. and Still, S., (1993). Hollibrook Accelerated Elementary School. In J. Murphy and P. Hallinger (Eds.), *Restructuring schools: Learning from ongoing efforts.* Newbury Park, CA: Corwin.

Meier, D. (1987). Central Park East: An alternative story. *Phi Delta Kappan, 68*,10, 753-757.

Monthly Business Failures. (1991a). Business failures increase 39 percent in October. Vol. *33*(10).

Monthly Business Failures. (1991b). New business increase 2.1 percent in October. Vol. *33*(10).

National Center for Education Statistics. (1992). *Digest of education statistics* (U.S. DOE Publication NCES 92-097). Washington, DC: U.S. Government Printing Office.

National Coalition for the Homeless. (1987). *Broken lives: Denial of education to the homeless.* Washington, DC.

National Commission on Excellence in Education. (1983). *A nation at risk: The imperative for educational reform.* Washington, DC: U.S. Department of Education.

Newman, F. M. (1991). What is a restructured school? A framework to clarify means and ends. *Issues in Restructuring Schools, 1*, 3-5, 16.

Oakes, J. (1985). *Keeping track: How schools structure inequity.* New Haven, CT: Yale University Press.

Peterson, J. M. (1989). Remediation is no remedy. *Educational Leadership, 46*(5), 24-25.

Quarterly Economic Report on Small Business. (1991, Fall). Index of small business optimism. Vol. *73*, 22-23.

Reich, R. B. (1991). *The work of nations: Preparing ourselves for 21st century capitalism.* New York: Alfred A. Knopf.

Reynolds, A. (1992, March 12). The middle class boom of the 1980s. *Wall Street Journal*, p. A12.

Sarason, S. B. (1982). *Culture of the school and the problem of changes.* Boston: Allyn and Bacon.

Shanker, A. (June 15, 1993). A speech to the National Science Foundation in Washington, DC.

Slavin, R. E. (1987). Ability grouping and student achievement in elementary schools: A best-evidence synthesis. *Review of Educational Research, 57*, 293-336.

Slavin, R. E. (1990). Achievement effects of ability grouping in secondary schools: A best-evidence synthesis. *Review of Educational Research, 60*, 471-499.

Smith, M., et al. (1992). State policy and systemic school reform. *Educational Technology, 32*(11): 31-36.

Stenmark, J. K., Thompson, V., and Cossey, R. (1986). *Family math.* Berkeley: University of California, Lawrence Hall of Science.

Stevenson, H. W. (1987). The Asian advantage: The case of mathematics. *American Educator: The Professional Journal of the American Federation of Teachers, 11*(2), 26-31.

Stevenson, H. W. (1990). *Making the grade in mathematics: Elementary school mathematics in the United States, Taiwan, and Japan.* Reston, VA: National Council of Teachers of Mathematics. (ERIC Document Reproduction Service No. ED 319 592)

Stevenson, H. W. (1992). "Learning from Asian Schools." *Scientific American. 267*(6): 70-76.

U.S. Bureau of the Census. (1992). *Statistical abstract of the United States* (112th ed.). Washington, DC: U.S. Government Printing Office.

U.S. Department of Education. (1988). *Digest of educational statistics.* Washington, DC: U.S. Government Printing Office.

U.S. Department of Education. (1991). *America 2000: An education strategy.* Washington, DC: U.S. Government Printing Office.

U.S. Department of Labor, Bureau of Labor Statistics. (1992). *Counting the unemployed* [Press release]. Washington, DC: U.S. Government Printing Office.

Walter, J. (1991) [High school graduation rate and post-secondary school attendance rate]. Unpublished raw data.

Willms, J. D. (1985). Catholic-school effects on academic achievement: New evidence from the high school and beyond follow-up study. *Sociology of Education. 58*(2): 98-114.

Working Groups of the Commission on Standards for School Mathematics of the National Council of Teachers of Mathematics. (1989). *Curriculum and evaluation standards for school mathematics.* Reston, VA: National Council of Teachers of Mathematics.

About the Editors and Contributors

Editors

Cheryl L. Fagnano is vice president for educational programs and administration at the Milken Institute for Job & Capital Formation. She previously served as executive assistant to Dr. Lewis C. Solmon in his capacity as dean of the Graduate School of Education at UCLA. Dr. Fagnano has coauthored several articles with Dr. Solmon on teaching testing programs and faculty hiring practices. She received her doctorate in education from the University of California, Los Angeles.

Katherine Nouri Hughes is director of communications for the Foundations of the Milken Families. She was previously a vice president at the strategic communications firm of Robinson, Lake, Lerer & Montgomery in New York, and served at the American University in Cairo. She completed her undergraduate and graduate studies at Princeton University, where she received her master of arts degree in Near Eastern Studies.

Keynote Speakers

Chester E. Finn, Jr., is professor of education and public policy at Vanderbilt University and director of the Educational Excellence Network, based in the university's Washington office. He is also a senior fellow of the Vanderbilt Institute for Public Policy Studies and a strategist on the Edison Project of Whittle Communications. In addition to his professorate, Dr. Finn served as a consultant to former Education Secretary Lamar Alexander and assisted in planning the America 2000 strategy. He is also president of the Madison Center for Educational Affairs and adjunct senior fellow at the Hudson Institute. His prior positions include staff assistant to the president of the United States, committee member of the President's Education Policy Advisory Committee, counsel of the American ambassador to India, research associate in governmental studies at the Brookings Institution, and legislative director for Senator Daniel P. Moynihan. The most recent of his seven books is *We Must Take Charge: Our Schools and Our Future,* published by the Free

Press in May 1991. In addition to an undergraduate degree in American history and a master's degree in social studies, Dr. Finn holds a doctorate in education policy and administration from Harvard University.

Henry M. Levin is professor of education and affiliated professor of economics at Stanford University, where he also serves as director of the Center for Education Research at Stanford (CERAS). Prior to his arrival at Stanford in 1968, Dr. Levin was a research associate in the Economic Studies Division of the Brookings Institution. Dr. Levin is a specialist in the economics of education and human resources. His work has focused specifically on cost-effectiveness, educational finance, and educational requirements of high technologies and investment strategies for educationally at-risk students. Much of his recent work addresses the establishment of schools designed to accelerate the learning of disadvantaged youngsters in order to bring them into the educational mainstream by the end of elementary school. Dr. Levin is editor of the *Review of Educational Research,* as well as the author of 11 books and more than 200 scholarly articles. He received his B.S. from New York University in 1960 and his master's and doctorate degrees from Rutgers University in 1962 and 1967, respectively.

Contributors

Gordon M. Ambach is the executive director of the Council of Chief State School Officers in Washington, D.C. He previously served as the New York State commissioner of education and as president of the State University of New York. In his current position, Mr. Ambach represents all of the state commissioners and superintendents of education as advocate for their state and national education policies and directs their council offices. Mr. Ambach's career, which includes teaching at the secondary and collegiate levels and the presidency of a local teacher's association, has centered on education policy making and legislative de-velopment, with a special focus on the sharing of local, state, and federal government responsibility. He currently serves on advisory commissions addressing topics as diverse as learning technology, international comparative studies of education, the arts, the Job Training Partnership Act, and education statistics and assessment. A graduate of Yale University, Mr. Ambach received a degree in teaching from Harvard University.

Linton Deck is director of education and nonprofit sector applications at the Center for Creative Leadership in Greensboro, North Carolina. Formerly a superintendent of schools in Fairfax County, Virginia; Orange County, Florida; and Bibb County, Georgia, Dr. Deck began his professional career in Atlanta as a science teacher, football coach, and high school principal. Dr. Deck came to the Center for Creative Leadership from Vanderbilt University, where he was chairman of the Department of Educational Leadership and founding director of the Center for the Advanced Study of Educational Leadership. His research has examined the office of the superintendent, and he is developing a national video archive of interviews with educational chief executive officers. Dr. Deck also serves as a consultant to school districts, state departments of education, corporations serving educational organizations, and the U.S. Department of Education. In addition to an undergraduate degree from Davidson College and a master of arts degree from Vanderbilt University, he received his doctorate in education from Harvard University.

Linda Darling-Hammond is professor of education at Teachers College, Columbia University, and co-director of the National Center for Restructuring Education, Schools and Teaching (NCREST). She is internationally recognized for her work in educational policy research, particularly in the areas of teaching and educational equity. Dr. Darling-Hammond's recent work has included studies of teacher evaluation and selection practices, teacher supply and demand, teacher education and certification, inequalities in students' educational opportunities, the development of educational indicators, accountability and assessment, and school restructuring. She is editor of the *Review of Research in Education* and coeditor of *The New Handbook of Teacher Evaluation*, and has served on the editorial advisory boards of *Education Researcher* and the *American Journal of Education*. She also serves on the executive board of the American Education Research Association. Dr. Darling-Hammond received her B.A. from Yale University and her doctorate in urban education from Temple University in 1978. Her many honors include the Phi Delta Kappa George E. Walk Award for the most outstanding dis-sertation in the field of education (1978), the American Education Research Association's Research Review Award, the American Federation of Teachers' Quest Award for Outstanding Scholarship, and the Association of Teacher Educators' Leadership Education Award.

Lowell Milken is a co-founder of the Foundations of the Milken Families and has served as president since their inception in 1982. Mr. Milken formulated the Foundations' missions in the areas of education, community services, health care and medical research and human welfare. In addition to conceiving and implementing innovative programs with his brother in all the Foundations' giving areas, he has been responsible for the expansion nationwide of a number of these programs. Mr. Milken has held positions of distinction in both the legal profession and the financial community. He graduated summa cum laude and Phi Beta Kappa from the University of California, Berkeley, and received his law degree from the University of California, Los Angeles Law School, having served as an editor on the *UCLA Law Review* and with the distinction of the Order of the Coif.

Valerie Mills chairs the Mathematics Department at Ypsilanti High School and is district math coordinator in Ypsilanti, Michigan. She is also an adjunct lecturer at the University of Michigan. Ms. Mills has helped develop numerous programs, partnerships, and curricula throughout Michigan, including Math Unlimited and the Math & Science Think Tank, a task force that inspires minorities and women to complete advanced classes in math and science. Ms. Mills has had a significant role in integrating computer technology into the school curriculum, and in writing items for the tenth-grade State of Michigan Assessment Test. Ms. Mills is a recipient of the Presidential Award for Excellence in Science and Math Teaching and a 1990 recipient of the Milken Family Foundation National Educator Award. She received her B.A. in mathematics and a master of arts degree in guidance and counseling from Eastern Michigan University.

Lewis C. Solmon is President of the Milken Institute for Job & Capital Formation. An economist and an educator, Dr. Solmon not only leads the Institute but is also responsible for the education component of the Milken Family Foundation National Education Conference. Dr. Solmon, who was formerly Dean of UCLA's Graduate School of Education, has published more than a score of books and monographs and over 60 scholarly articles. He earned his undergraduate degree at the University of Toronto and took his master's and doctoral degrees in economics at the University of Chicago.

Milken Family Foundation National Educator Award Recipients 1987–1991*

Award Recipient	Position/School	State	Year
Carolyn Lott Adams	Principal & Attendance Ctr. Administrator *Oak Grove Schools*	Mississippi	1991
E. Norlene Adams	Teacher *Northside Elementary*	Nevada	1991
Katherine Afendoulis	Teacher *Meadow Brook*	Michigan	1991
Lea Albert	Principal *Kahuku High & Intermediate School*	Hawaii	1990
Margaret Allan	Teacher *Greenville Jr. High School*	Illinois	1988
Janet S. Allen	Professor of Literary Eucation *University of Central Florida*	Maine	1991
Jorge Alvarez	Teacher *Central High School*	Rhode Island	1991
Roberta Ameen	Teacher *NICE Community Schools*	Michigan	1990
Deborah Anderson	Asst. Principal *Walter S. Christopher School*	Illinois	1989
Evie Andrews	Teacher *Tualatin Elementary School*	Oregon	1990
Neil Anstead	Coordinator/Teacher *Grover Cleveland High School*	California	1987
Delia Armstrong-Busby	Principal *Mitchell High School*	Colorado	1990
James Aseltine	Principal *Irving A. Robbins Middle School*	Connecticut	1989

* Milken Family Foundation National Educator Awards are announced in the Fall; the Retreat—now "Conference"—is held annually the following Spring.

Award Recipient	Position/School	State	Year
Steven Asheim	Teacher *Heritage High School*	Colorado	1991
Ede Ashworth	Teacher *Brooke High School*	West Virginia	1990
Elizabeth Asteriadis	Instructor *Glenn Hare Center*	Nevada	1991
Alfred Balasco	Teacher *Smithfield High School*	Rhode Island	1990
James Barlow	Teacher *Aloha High School*	Oregon	1990
Edward Barrett	Principal *Analy High School*	California	1991
Linda Bates-Transou	Principal *Manual High School*	Colorado	1989
Barrie Becker	Teacher *Dorothy Kirby Center*	California	1989
Patricia Bell	Teacher *Shepardson Elementary School*	Colorado	1989
Sharon Belshaw-Jones	Principal *Fremont Unified School Disrict*	California	1988
Deveria A. Berry	Teacher *Martin Luther King Jr. Elementary School*	Connecticut	1991
Felica Ann Bryan Bessent	Teacher *Valley High School*	California	1991
Leslie Bettencourt	Teacher *Lincoln Jr./Sr. High School*	Rhode Island	1991
John Blaydes	Principal *J. H. McGaugh High School*	California	1988
Jill Board	Teacher *Oakridge Elementary School*	Oregon	1991
Jewell Boutte	Program Manager *San Francisco State University*	California	1988
Charles Bowen	Principal *Broadmoor Jr. High School*	Illinois	1988
Paul Bowen	Teacher *Petersburg High School*	Alaska	1990
Sheila Bowens	Teacher *Hamel Elementary School*	Illinois	1990
Rosemarye Boykins	Teacher *J.K. Harper*	Georgia	1991
Bernard Bradley	Science Specialist *Newberry Math and Science Academy*	Illinois	1991

Award Recipient	Position/School	State	Year
William Branch	Teacher *Evanston Township High School*	Illinois	1990
John Breaugh	Principal *Marvin Beekman Center*	Michigan	1991
Kathleen Brendza	Administrator *The Center*	Colorado	1991
Ronald Bright	Teacher-Coordinator *Castle High School*	Hawaii	1990
Cynthia Ann Broad	Teacher Consultant *Lobbestael Elementary School*	Michigan	1990
Sharon Brock	Principal *Boynton Elementary School*	Georgia	1990
Deb A. Brown	Teacher *Lakewood Elementary*	West Virginia	1991
Frank Brusa	Principal *Las Vegas High School*	Nevada	1991
James Bryn	Teacher *Sparks High School*	Nevada	1990
Linda Bunch	Teacher *Independence Valley Elementary School*	Nevada	1988
Jean Burkus	Teacher *Amity Regional Jr. High School*	Connecticut	1989
Susan Burt	Librarian/Teacher *Marlinton Middle School*	West Virginia	1990
Janie Pressley Butts	Teacher *Flanders Elementary School*	Connecticut	1990
Betty Campbell	Principal *Boise-Eliot Elementary*	Oregon	1991
Joyce Carey	Teacher *Benjamin Franklin School*	Illinois	1989
Ronald Carter	Teacher *East St. Louis High School*	Illinois	1991
Michael Cassity	Learning Center Coordinator *Feather River Community College*	California	1988
Francis Chamberlain	Director of Instruction *Napa County Office of Education*	California	1987
Yvonne Chan	Principal *Vaughn Elementary School*	California	1991
Phyllis Cheaney	Principal *Lincoln School*	Illinois	1989
Walter J. Clark	Principal *Blatchley Middle School*	Alaska	1991

Award Recipient	Position/School	State	Year
Elizabeth Clemons	Teacher *Creekside Elementary*	Illinois	1989
Dora Cline	Teacher *Dillingham High School*	Alaska	1990
Margaret Clinkscales	Teacher *High Horizons Magnet School*	Connecticut	1988
Lois Cohn	Librarian/Teacher *McGaugh School*	California	1991
Frances Coleman	Teacher *Ackerman High School and Weir A.C.*	Mississippi	1991
Louise Coleman	Superintendent *Taft School*	Illinois	1989
Christine Comins	Teacher *Pueblo County High School*	Colorado	1989
Jeannette Condon	Principal *Fort Fairfield Elementary School*	Maine	1990
Steve Connolly	Teacher *Cloverdale High School*	California	1987
Teresa Corpuz	Principal *Albany Middle School*	California	1987
Rose Cousar	Teacher *Screven County High School*	Georgia	1990
Robert Cross	Principal *Century High School*	Illinois	1989
Rosemary Culverwell	Principal *Reilly School*	Illinois	1991
Mary Curtiss	Teacher *Trumbull High School*	Connecticut	1990
Joan D'Agostino	Teacher *Mt. Desert Island High School*	Maine	1990
Janet Daijogo	Teacher *Marin Country Day Elementary School*	California	1990
Dan Daniel	Teacher *Parkersburg High School*	West Virginia	1991
Phyllis Darling	Social Studies Curriculum Specialist *Clark County School District*	Nevada	1991
Edward Davis	Principal *Weaver High School*	Connecticut	1990
Jeanne E. Dawson	Teacher *Edward S. Rodes Elementary School*	Rhode Island	1990

Award Recipient	Position/School	State	Year
Teresa de Garcia	Teacher *University Hill Elementary School*	Colorado	1989
Francey Dennis	Principal *Silver Lake Elementary School*	Nevada	1989
David Dierking	Principal *Will C. Wood Middle School*	California	1991
Larry Dorsey-Spitz	Teacher *Hellbeck Elementary*	Colorado	1991
Richard DuFour	District Superintendent *District 125*	Illinois	1988
John Duncan	Principal *Elderberry Elementary School*	California	1989
Robert Dyer	Teacher *Sea Road School*	Maine	1990
William V. Edwards	Principal *Cimarron-Memorial High School*	Nevada	1988
Stephen C. Ellwood IV	Teacher *St. Francis Elementary School*	Maine	1991
Dorthey Felicetti	Principal *Wilson School*	Illinois	1990
Francine C. Fernandez	Principal *Kailua Elementary*	Hawaii	1991
Bruce Fisher	Teacher *Fortuna Elementary*	California	1991
Cheryl Fisher-Allen	Teacher *Gilbert Stewart School*	Rhode Island	1990
Anita Fisk	Asst. Principal *Pershing County Jr.-Sr. High School*	Nevada	1988
Donna M. Fitzgerald	Asst. Principal & Teacher *Illing Middle School*	Connecticut	1991
Delores Aaron Flagg	Teacher *Blanchette Middle School*	Michigan	1991
James Ford	Principal *Henry D. Sheldon High School*	Oregon	1990
Malinda Frazier	Teacher *Lovelock Elementary School*	Nevada	1990
Claire Furukawa	Teacher *Kalani High School*	Hawaii	1991
Janis T. Gabay	Teacher *Junipero Serra High School*	California	1990
Don Gabriel	Teacher *Brush High School*	Colorado	1991

Award Recipient	Position/School	State	Year
Teresa Gallman	Teacher *Woodbine Elementary School*	Georgia	1990
Elizabeth Garand	Teacher *Northwest Middle School*	Connecticut	1988
Gaylon Garner	Teacher *Ralph H. Metcalfe Magnet School*	Illinois	1988
Norma Garnett	Teacher *Toll Gate High School*	Rhode Island	1990
Frank D. Gawle	Teacher *Enfield High School*	Connecticut	1990
Jancie Gehrman	Teacher *William H. Brown School*	Illinois	1990
John Genasci	Principal *Sparks Middle School*	Nevada	1988
Shirley Gillis	Teacher *Harbor School*	Connecticut	1989
Larry Ginoza	Teacher *Waiane High School*	Hawaii	1991
Eula Mae Glenn	Teacher *Pelham Middle School*	Michigan	1991
Pamela Granucci	Principal *Lincoln School*	Connecticut	1989
Patricia Grimmer	Teacher *Carbondale High School*	Illinois	1989
Mario Guerrero	Teacher *Jackson Elementary School*	California	1991
Lynne Haeffele	Math & Science Supervisor *Bloomington High School*	Illinois	1988
Thomas Hall	Teacher *Colquitt High School*	Georgia	1990
Timothy Harvey	Principal *William E. Fanning Elementary School*	California	1990
LeRoy E. Hay	Acting Superintendent *East Lyme Public School*	Connecticut	1988
Sandee Gilletti Hay	Director, Federal Programs *Evans Elementary School*	Colorado	1990
David S. Heckman	Teacher *Monmouth Academy*	Maine	1991
Suzanne Henning	Teacher *Tanana School*	Alaska	1990
Margarita C. Hernandez	Principal *Burton Elementary School*	Michigan	1990

Award Recipient	Position/School	State	Year
James Hieftje	Principal *Fremont Middle School*	Michigan	1990
Peter Hodges	Principal *Alicia Reyes Elementary School*	California	1989
Herbert Holland	Teacher *Crenshaw High School*	California	1990
Fred Horlacher	Teacher *Reed High School*	Nevada	1989
Nancy Housand	Teacher *Wynnton Elementary School*	Georgia	1991
Edward Howland	Teacher *Shasta High School*	California	1991
Richard A. Hunsaker	Teacher *Belleville West High School*	Illinois	1990
John Hurley	Asst. District Superintendent *Harlem Consolidated Schools*	Illinois	1990
Amy Ish	Teacher *El Gabilan School*	California	1989
Edward M. Jacomo	Principal *Friends School*	Michigan	1991
Mae C. Johnson	Principal *Monterey High School*	California	1987
Cherry J.M. Jones	Principal & Professor *Flanders Elementary School*	Connecticut	1991
Louise C. Jones	Principal *George Washington Carver Elementary School*	California	1990
Mark Jordan	Teacher & Administrator *Gompers Fine Arts Option School*	Illinois	1989
Edward C. Keller III	Teacher *Mountainview Elementary School*	West Virginia	1990
M. Marjorie Kellogg	Teacher *Marietta High School*	Georgia	1991
Michael Klippert	Teacher *River Ridge Middle School*	Illinois	1991
Jack Knuston	Teacher *Plateau Valley High School*	Colorado	1991
Thomas Koeningsberger	Teacher *Guilford High School*	Illinois	1988
Jacqueline Kookesh	Teacher *Angoon School*	Alaska	1991
Roberta Koss	Teacher *Redwood High School*	California	1990

Award Recipient	Position/School	State	Year
Peter Krasa	Principal *La Mesa Elementary*	California	1991
Leonora T. Kunimoto	Principal *Waiakea High School*	Hawaii	1991
William Langley	Principal *St. Viator School*	Nevada	1990
Daniel Lawson	Region Administrator *LAUSD; Elementary-District A*	California	1991
Mary Laycock	Math Specialist *Nueva Center for Learning*	California	1989
Margaret Leeds	Asst. Principal *Beverly Hills High School*	California	1987
Judith Essex Leonard	Teacher *Southern RI Regional Collaborative*	Rhode Island	1991
William LePore	Teacher *Crater High School*	Oregon	1991
Richard Lindgren	Retired Principal & Professor Central CT State University *Illing Jr. High School*	Connecticut	1988
Craig Lindvahl	Music Director *Teutopolis Grade School*	Illinois	1989
Jerry Linkinoggor	Principal *Clay County High School*	West Virginia	1990
Irene W. Llewellyn	Teacher *Laurel Elementary*	Connecticut	1991
Robert Lowry	Principal *Raymond J. Fisher Jr. High School*	California	1989
Charles Lutgen	Principal *Woodland Park Middle School*	Colorado	1990
George R. Mansfield	Executive Director *Educational Services Center*	Colorado	1991
Patrick Mara	Teacher *South High School*	Colorado	1990
Patricia C. Marden	Teacher *Belleview Elementary*	Colorado	1991
Chiyomi Masuda	Teacher *Albany Middle School*	California	1991
Jeniane Gee Matt	Teacher *Christine Sipherd Elementary School*	California	1989
Joseph Mattos	Principal *James H. Bean Elementary School*	Maine	1990

Award Recipient	Position/School	State	Year
Gene McCallum	Administrator *Middle Schools Unity*	California	1987
Kevin McCann	Principal *Jamieson Elementary School*	Illinois	1990
Clyde McGrady	Principal *Staley Middle School*	Georgia	1990
Rae Ellen McKee	Teacher *Slanesville Elementary School*	West Virginia	1991
Charolette Meade	Teacher *Monogah Middle School*	West Virginia	1991
Robert Mellette	Program Director *Betsy Ross Magnet School*	Connecticut	1988
Paul Mello	Teacher *Middletown High School*	Rhode Island	1990
Marjorie Miller	Teacher *Longfellow School*	Maine	1991
Winnie Miller	Teacher *Lake Oswego Jr. High*	Oregon	1991
Valerie Mills	Teacher *Ypsilanti High School*	Michigan	1990
Yvonne Minor	Principal *Walter H. Dyett School*	Illinois	1990
Tamiko Jobe Miyagi	Teacher *Academy for Math and Science*	Nevada	1991
Jean Miyahara	Technology Learning Center Coordinator *Waipahu High School*	Hawaii	1990
Cynthia Montoya	Librarian *James Gibson Elementary School*	Nevada	1990
Cosetta Moore	Independent Consultant *LA Unified School District*	California	1989
Roger Moore	Principal *Lake City Elementary*	Michigan	1991
Roger Morrissette	Teacher *Sedgwick Middle School*	Connecticut	1989
Norma Mota-Altman	Teacher *Emery Park Elementary School*	California	1990
Larry Moye	Teacher *Soltdana High School*	Alaska	1990
Ralph Murakami	Deputy District Superintendent *Department of Education*	Hawaii	1990

Award Recipient	Position/School	State	Year
Connie Murphree	Teacher *Olive Branch Middle School*	Mississippi	1991
Irene Murphy	Principal *Mason Elementary School*	West Virginia	1991
Linda Murray	Teacher *Hyde Park Career Academy*	Illinois	1988
Darrell Myers	Teacher *Zane Jr. High School*	California	1989
Richard B. Nabel	Principal *Naugatuck High School*	Connecticut	1991
Lorna Mae Nagata	Principal *Mulberry Elementary School*	California	1988
Sharon Nakagawa	Principal *Waialua Elementary School*	Hawaii	1991
Nena Nanfeldt	Principal *Nathan Hale School*	Connecticut	1988
William Nave	Teacher/Coordinator *Regional Alternative Program*	Maine	1990
Karen Nemetz	Principal *Mission Avenue Open School*	California	1989
Bert Neumaier	Teacher *Farmington Public Schools*	Connecticut	1991
Barbra Neureither	Teacher *Holt High School*	Michigan	1991
David Neves	Teacher *Scituate Jr./Sr. High School*	Rhode Island	1991
Robert Nunez	Teacher *Eisenhower Middle School*	Illinois	1991
Philip Ogata	Teacher *Boulder High School*	Colorado	1990
Pamela Ogle	Teacher & Consultant *Waverly East Intermediate*	Michigan	1991
Mary Omberg	Teacher *Nyssa High School*	Oregon	1990
Steven Parker	Principal *Joaquin Miller Jr. High School*	California	1990
Judith Pavlak	Teacher *Channing Memorial Elementary School*	Illinois	1990
Arthur Peekel	Teacher *Rolling Meadows High School*	Illinois	1991
Steven Pellegrini	Teacher *Yerington High School*	Nevada	1990

Award Recipient	Position/School	State	Year
Louise Pempek	Teacher *Putnam Public Schools*	Connecticut	1989
Philip Perez	Deputy Superintendent of Instr. Services *Riverside Unified School District*	California	1988
Wayne Piercy	Director of Legislative Services *Long Beach Unified School District*	California	1990
Klaire Pirtle	Principal *Kingsbury Middle School*	Nevada	1988
Larry Plew	Superintendent & Principal *Trinity Union High School Disrict*	California	1990
Linda Poff	Teacher *Straley Elementary School*	West Virginia	1990
Diane Price-Stone	Teacher *Philomath Elementary School*	Oregon	1990
John Putnam	Teacher *Washington Irving Jr. High School*	Colorado	1989
Nelson W. Quinby III	Principal *Joel Barlow High School*	Connecticut	1989
Virginia Rebar	Principal *Haddam-Killingworth Middle School*	Connecticut	1990
Daniel Record	Teacher *Portland High School*	Connecticut	1990
Arthur Reisman	Teacher *East Leyden High School*	Illinois	1989
Margaret Reynolds	Teacher *Park View School*	Illinois	1990
Gayle Richter	Teacher *Zion-Benton High School*	Illinois	1989
Thomas Ridgeway	Teacher *Georgia Academy for the Blind*	Georgia	1990
Donald Ring	Lecturer of Secondary School Methods *Trinity College*	Illinois	1991
Lucia Rivera	Principal *Bradford Elementary School*	Colorado	1989
Doris Robertson	Director of Grant Development *Fulton County Schools*	Georgia	1990
Sandra Robinson	Interim Superintendent *Detroit Public Schools – Area D*	Michigan	1990
Michael Rodriguez	Counselor *Lee High School*	Arkansas	1991

Award Recipient	Position/School	State	Year
Pamela Rolfe	Teacher *Limestone Jr.-Sr. High School*	Maine	1990
Larry D. Romine	Teacher *Lamar Middle School*	Colorado	1991
Elaine Rosenfield	Teacher *Sinsheimer Elementary School*	California	1987
Shirly Rosenkranz	Teacher *Temple City High School*	California	1987
James Roth	Teacher *Riverwood Elementary School*	Illinois	1990
Barbra S. Rous	Project Director *Director of Individualized Arts Program*	Georgia	1991
Patricia Rowe	Teacher *Lovelock Elementary School*	Nevada	1989
Kenneth Roy	Curriculum Director *Glastonbury Public Schools*	Connecticut	1989
Ruthanne Rust	Teacher *Denali Elementary School*	Alaska	1991
Donna Saiki	Principal *Hilo High School*	Hawaii	1990
Jennifer Salls	Coordinator *Bullis Curriculum & Instruction Center*	Nevada	1989
Drexel Sammons	Teacher *Crescent Elementary School*	West Virginia	1991
Carol Samsel	Teacher *Smalley Elementary School*	Connecticut	1990
Richard Sander	Teacher *Ketchikan High School*	Alaska	1991
Julia Sanders	Teacher *Pulaski County Elementary School*	Georgia	1991
Rhonda Schier	Teacher *Ponderosa Elementary School*	Colorado	1989
Edward Schroeder	Teacher *Coolidge Jr. High School*	Illinois	1988
Stewart Schultz	Teacher *GMI Engineering Management Institute*	Michigan	1990
Charles Etta Scott	Asst. Principal *Waycross High School*	Georgia	1991
Rodolpho Serna	Asst. Superintendent *Chicago Public Schools*	Illinois	1989
Virgil Sestini	Teacher *The Meadows School*	Nevada	1989

Award Recipient	Position/School	State	Year
Thomas J. Sferes	Teacher *Kennebunk High School*	Maine	1991
Sylvia Shaina	Teacher *Thomas Edison Elementary School*	Michigan	1990
Kathy Sheiko	Principal *Green Elementary School*	Michigan	1991
Doris Shipp	Teacher *Doris Reed Elementary School*	Nevada	1988
Milton Shishido	Principal *Waipahu High School*	Hawaii	1991
James Simmons	Principal *Nelson Wilks Elementary School*	Arkansas	1991
Blanche F. Smith	Teacher *Decatur Classical School*	Illinois	1991
Paula Smith	Teacher *Washington Elementary School*	Arkansas	1991
Robert Smith	Principal *South Kingstown Jr. High School*	Rhode Island	1990
Sanderson Smith	Teacher *Cate School*	California	1988
Allan G. Snell	Principal & Curriculum Director *Washington Street School*	Maine	1991
Margo Sorenson	Teacher *Harbor Day School*	California	1991
Dwight Souers	Teacher *Willamette High School*	Oregon	1990
Carol Sparks	Teacher *Foothill Middle School*	California	1987
Shirley Splittstoesser	Teacher *Wiley Elementary School*	Illinois	1990
Randy Steinheimer	Teacher *J. H. Freeman Elementary School*	Illinois	1988
Vivian Stephens	Teacher *Clairemont Elementary School*	Georgia	1990
Susan Stitham	Teacher *Lathrop High School*	Alaska	1991
Tom Stone	Teacher *Sheldon High School*	Oregon	1991
Floyd Sucher	Professor of Elementary Education *Brigham Young University*	Alaska	1990

Award Recipient	Position/School	State	Year
Harriss E. Sullivan, Jr.	Principal *Evans High School*	Georgia	1991
Marie Sullivan	Teacher *Sabin Jr. High School*	Colorado	1990
Thomas Sullivan	Teacher *Valley Regional High School*	Connecticut	1988
Bertha Sutton	Principal *Monte Sano Elementary*	Georgia	1991
Jeffery Swenerton	Principal *Carmel Del Mar School*	California	1987
Patricia Swinton	Teacher *Provine High School*	Mississippi	1991
Wayne Tanaka	Principal *Clark High School*	Nevada	1989
Harold Taylor	Teacher *Lincoln Early & Middle Elementary School*	Michigan	1990
Jean Tello	Teacher *A. A. Stagg High School*	Illinois	1988
Philip Terrell	District Superintendent *Pass Christian Public School District*	Mississippi	1991
Herman L. Thomas	Asst. Superintendent *Arkadelphia Public Schools*	Arkansas	1991
Jane Thompson	Principal *Palisades School*	Illinois	1988
Lynn Thompson	Teacher *Peoria Development Center*	Illinois	1991
Yvonne Toma	Teacher *Kipapa Elementary School*	Hawaii	1990
Nancy Toupal	Teacher *East Street Elementary School*	Colorado	1990
Judy Trumble	Teacher *Edison School*	Illinois	1991
Joan Turner	Teacher *Matt Kelly Sixth Grade Center*	Nevada	1990
Phyllis Turner	Teacher *Monroe Elementary School*	California	1990
Jose Valderas	Director of Compensatory Education Progams *Dolsen Center*	Michigan	1991
John Vallino	Teacher *DeSoto Elementary School*	Illinois	1991

Award Recipient	Position/School	State	Year
Susan Van Zant	Principal *Morning Creek School*	California	1989
David Vigilante	Consultant *Gompers Secondary School*	California	1988
Carol R. Virostek	Teacher *Berlin High School*	Connecticut	1991
Patricia Walker	Teacher *Bloom Trail High School*	Illinois	1991
Robert Wallace	District Superintendent *Cumberland School Department*	Rhode Island	1991
Darlene Walsh	Teacher *Greenbush Elementary School*	Rhode Island	1991
Sidney Weathermon	Teacher *Martin Park Elementary School*	Colorado	1990
Carol R. Wheeler	Principal *Buckley School*	Connecticut	1990
Marilyn Whirry	Teacher *Mira Costa High School*	California	1988
Jeffrey White	Teacher *Trickum Middle School*	Georgia	1991
Debra White-Hunt	Teacher *Detroit-Windsor Dance Academy*	Michigan	1990
Lore Wiggins	Teacher *Gateway High School*	Colorado	1989
Kim Bridger Wilbanks	Asst. Principal *Fox Meadow Elementary School*	Arkansas	1991
Virgil Wilkins	Teacher *Hundred High School*	West Virginia	1990
Deborah Willard	Director of Social Studies *Glastonbury Board of Education*	Connecticut	1988
Gordon M. Williams	Teacher *Trumbull High School*	Connecticut	1991
Jean Williams	Foreign Language Coordinator *Carrollton City Elementary School*	Georgia	1990
Thomas Williams	Teacher *Fayetteville High School*	Arkansas	1991
Vee Wilson	Principal *Grant Bowler Elementary*	Nevada	1991
Edward Wong	Teacher *Vicksburg High School*	Mississippi	1991
Wilton Wong	Teacher *Capuchino High School*	California	1990

Award Recipient	**Position/School**	**State**	**Year**
Harriet L. Woodard	Teacher *Stone Mountain Jr. High School*	Georgia	1991
Deanna Gael Woods	Teacher *Wilson High School*	Oregon	1991
Donna York	Teacher *Romig Jr. High School*	Alaska	1991

Index

About the Book

Beginning with the fundamental and essential question, "How do we improve schools?" prominent education theorists and practitioners examine the imperative of education reform. They confront and analyze the pressing need for effective, systematic ways to improve education in order to ensure competent students and graduates, and they offer numerous innovative ideas and models for reform.

The discussions in this book are the fruits of the 1992 Milken Family Foundation National Educator Awards Retreat. Committed to recognizing the contributions of educators, the annual conference advances professional development and celebrates—publicly—professional achievement. Addressed in this volume are such urgent and far-reaching issues as enrichment versus remedial strategies for at-risk students; educators' responses to extra-education demands; creative leadership among practitioners; and the crucial role of educator awards. Practitioners, policymakers, and anyone wanting to stay current with the state of American education will find this useful and valuable reading.